SMALL GARDENS

AND BACKYARDS

DAVID STEVENS

CONRAN OCTOPUS

First published in 1986 by
Conran Octopus Limited
37 Shelton Street
London WC2H 9HN

Copyright © Conran Octopus Limited 1986

Reprinted 1987, 1991, 1993 (twice)

Project Editor	Hilary Arnold
Art Editor	Stephen Bull
Designers	Mark Richards, Alan Marshall
Illustrators	Mulkern Rutherford Studio
Editors	Catherine Carpenter, Deborah Loth
Picture Researcher	Nadine Bazar
Production	Jill Embleton

ISBN 1 85029 065 2

Typeset by Text Filmsetters Limited

Printed and bound in Hong Kong

CONTENTS

GARDEN DESIGN

The problem with most books on design, and garden design in particular, is that they over-complicate what is essentially a simple subject. What is worse, they attribute to the designer some sort of magic whereby any successful composition is a spontaneous creation. Any designer worth his salt, and gardening is one area where there are many gifted amateurs, knows that a satisfactory result is usually achieved by following a well-tried formula that relies almost entirely on common sense.

For the first-time gardener, this problem can be compounded by keen botanists, horticulturalists and, to a lesser extent, by the media, who tend to be most enthusiastic about the newest blooms, vegetables and plants. The Latin terminology used to name plants can seem at times no more than a confusing way to explain how to grow bigger and duller varieties of plants on which ever more virulent pests survive.

This is not gardening at all, but rather an attitude likely to turn you off the subject for life.

Any small garden is really an extension of the home. The smaller that space the more important intelligent organization becomes. Gardening should not be hard work and you need never be a slave to what is essentially an oasis, particularly if it is set in the heart of a city.

As soon as you stop thinking of your backyard as an alien environment you will quickly be able to realize its full potential. What that potential is really depends on you. The danger in studying gardening books, and glossy magazines is the temptation simply to copy ideas.

Gardens are primarily concerned with personality – your personality – which is precisely why three identical plots will all turn out quite differently. If you approach planning your garden in the same way as any of the rooms inside the house you will not go far wrong. By doing this you will be able to plot circulation patterns, designate sitting areas, screen bad views or enhance good ones. Changes of level will be important, as will the demands of children, toys and pets. Remember the garden has to accept both the ugly and charming so bins, bikes, compost and rubbish will all need somewhere to go.

Take the time to make a careful list of all your requirements, beginning with the items listed at the end of the checklist opposite.

PLANNING CHECKLIST

- Have you carried out a survey of your garden (see page 19)?
- Are there any features you want to keep? Trees, shrubs, pools, paths, steps, fences, patio, barbecue?
- What sort of boundaries are there, if any? Fence, hedge, wall?
- Are there good or bad views to be emphasized or screened?
- Is there a change of level?
- Do prevailing winds or annoying draughts affect your site?
- How much sun do you get, and for how long, in different areas?
- Have you made a scale plan incorporating all the survey information (see page 20)?
- What is your budget?
- Are you competent at DIY construction?
- How much maintenance are you prepared to undertake?
- Have you listed your requirements? Do you need?
  - water supply
  - patio or deck
  - outdoor lighting
  - barbecue
  - garden furniture
  - shed
  - power points
  - play areas
  - containers
  - pool
  - greenhouse
  - garage

A garden often has to cater for everything and everybody – paving, paths, plants, pots, pool, lawn, children, pets, storage. This attractive little composition is simple and straightforward and works well for those who use it. The juxtaposition of planting frames the view from the window.

1 *This cheerful front garden has been designed as much for the pleasure of passers-by as for the private satisfaction of its owners. Many garden owners forget how much others genuinely appreciate their work. Here, maintenance has been kept to a minimum by installing simple brick paving instead of a lawn, which also provides a visual link with the adjoining building. This is matched by the sensible, slanted coping on top of the garden wall. Unfortunately, coping bricks such as these are not always available today.*
Colour is provided largely by annual plants, petunias and pelargoniums, which spill out of the troughs and beds. Climbing plants soften the house while the two tall conifers on either side of the window add an air of formality.

2 *Urban backyards can have an undeniable charm and this is the perfect outdoor room. The main garden is entered via a simple wrought-iron stair, which creates a particularly attractive split-level effect. Apart from the central sitting area, not a single square foot is devoid of plants. Pots and containers are used particularly well, even on the parapet wall. Crazy paving, although not always suitable for a small garden, is effective here, providing a low-key backdrop for the simple chairs and bamboo table.*

3 *Scale is important in a small garden and so too is an overall theme. This 'busy' design combines a number of elements with varying characteristics in a tiny area. The planting, however, acts as a soft green mantle that draws the composition together, provides continuity and screens the fence and protective netting of the local football ground which backs on to the yard.*

The simple green seat, which blends perfectly into the surrounding foliage and whose thin slats act as a foil to the bold pot opposite, is particularly effective. The arching palm frames the golden-leafed robinia in the background. Stepping stones reinforce the feeling of uniformity and here the random slabs are sensibly separated by washed gravel. An alternative treatment might have been to use grass, but maintenance would be difficult. Colour is perhaps the most important factor in a garden. Here, green is the dominant hue, with just a splash of red to lift the border beside the seat. Without this accent, the garden would be altogether too bland, mundane rather than pretty. Finally, this illustrates the effectiveness of an easily maintained utility lawn, as opposed to a lush bowling green. Zealous gardeners can waste countless hours on the lawn, and often the end result just is not worth it.

1 *A wooden deck by its very nature provides an ideal link with the surrounding landscape. Here, the naturally weathered timber platform seems to float against a gentle backdrop of trees. The awkward change in level has been handled by constructing a series of platforms. Furnishings are always desperately important and gardens should be made as comfortable as possible. Here, white is the overall theme, with a couple of pots of bright red geraniums and a paler yellow parasol in the background supplying an uplifting accent.*

2 *A view out of a garden is often indispensable, drawing the wider landscape into a more intimate setting. In this view, the landscape is framed by the simple loggia and sitting area beneath. The straightforward, unfussy furniture and floor do not detract from the setting. The variegated ivy wrapped around the massive pier complements the house.*

3 *This patio is very crisp, very modern and a real invitation outside. The grey carpet indoors and grey tiles of the terrace form an obvious link, while the vivid red furniture is even more striking against the dark paving. The background is low key, underlining the point that 'hot' colours most certainly draw the eye.*

4

4 *This simple, sheltered patio underlines one of the prime requirements of the backyard. The point is, of course, that such areas must be multi-purpose, serving a wide range of requirements. It does not really matter whether this is a front, back or side door: the space outside has been planned both to permit access and to provide a subsidiary sitting area. The table and built-in seating tuck neatly into a backwater alongside the main pedestrian flow into and out of the house.*

The feeling of enclosure is reinforced by the neatly detailed overhead canopy, which is softened by climbing plants. Such a canopy is ideal in this sort of situation, but be careful to roof it well. Although it might be tempting to use an inexpensive translucent material which would admit as much light as possible, corrugated plastic or fibreglass sheeting not only looks cheap, but also produces a noise like thunder in anything but the lightest shower. Better, as here, to paint all surfaces a bright white to reflect light. Potted pelargoniums and petunias introduce colour and can be moved about at random. The use of both statues and small pictures hanging on the walls outside makes this area seem even more like an indoor room and emphasizes the link between inside and out.

1 *The bare bones of this back-yard could have been not only dull, but downright ugly. The designer had to cope with a slightly ramshackle garage and an utterly nondescript space. The first step towards improvement was to paint the garage all one colour, thus minimizing the contrast between the different materials used in its construction and providing cohesion. White does the job best of all, not only because it reflects light into the small open area, but also because its brightness glosses over the awkward details between timber and brick.*

The choice of simple, neutral grey paving is particularly appropriate, and laying the slabs in a 'staggered' pattern helps to lead the eye down the space, giving an impression of movement and greater area. The furniture reinforces the bright, white theme, while a superb climbing white rose sprawls its way across the face of the spruced-up garage. The planting otherwise forms a soft envelope. Although this is a small space, there is still plenty of room for flowers and foliage. One great bonus of town gardens is the view into them from upstairs windows. Not only do you see them laid out as if on a drawing board, but you also see the surrounding landscape with the garden as your own sheltered oasis.

1

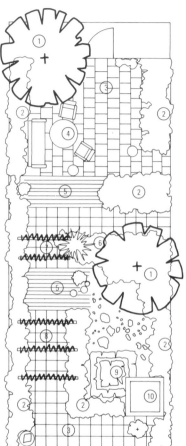

1

The plan of the backyard shown at left reveals how the owners have created an informal, secluded seating area in a sunny spot at the bottom. The long narrow shape of the plot has been broken up by a screen and planting.

1 Tree
2 Plants
3 Paving
4 Seating area
5 Brick paving
6 Screen
7 Arch
8 Pergola
9 Herb garden
10 Raised bed (for annuals)

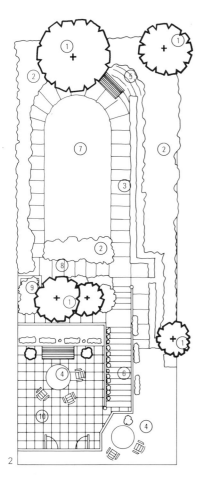

2

In the garden shown at right, change of level and hard landscaping, rather than planting, are used to create a shaded seating area near the house and a secluded retreat at the bottom of a long town garden in a warm climate.

1 Tree
2 Plants
3 Paving
4 Seating area
5 Brick paving
6 Change of level (stairs, railings)
7 Lawn
8 Path
9 Raised bed
10 Patio

2

2 *From an upstairs, bird's-eye perspective, the architecture of the surrounding townscape is very much drawn into the overall composition of this urban backyard. Although the lower patio, with its chequer-board paving, black table and white furniture, might seem too formal or clinical at first, it produces what is obviously a very personal space.*
There is a refreshing strength of purpose which is reinforced by the formal placement of all the components within the patio area. The long white seat takes pride of place and is flanked by a pair of white Versailles tubs planted with matching standard bays. Lighting is symmetrically but sensibly placed to illuminate the sitting area. Pink walls help to soften and warm the otherwise stark lower level. Steps climb to an upper terrace and here the mood is altogether different, with a mass of soft green foliage sweeping off into the more distant parts of the garden. Bright red geraniums introduce colour, and are placed so as to create a visual link between the lower patio and the upper terrace, which are otherwise quite different in style.
Visual continuity between the two levels is more subtly reinforced by central placement of the long seat in the formal, lower patio, which is echoed by the traditional bronze sculpture.

One of the most important rules of design is not to crystallize your ideas too soon. Take the time to complete the checklist on page 5, which will help you rationalize your planning sequence by quantifying your needs and analysing the physical characteristics of the plot. It will form the basis of a design that is right for you and could save ndless frustration later on.

Before you put pencil to paper you will also have needed to carry it an accurate survey, measuring the lengths of the boundaries, the mensions of the house, positions of doors and windows as well as ny features within the garden. Don't be tempted to rush out and remove anything that is immediately unsightly. While this may bring short-term satisfaction, it could be a costly mistake in design terms.

Other survey information will include the direction of any cold prevailing wind that will need screening, those good or bad views that we mentioned before, the type and condition of existing boundaries, neighbours, soil type and even the colour schemes of rooms adjoining the garden. A final vital factor and one that is all too often forgotten is the 'North Point', or the position of the sun in relation to your garden.

Once you have gathered all this information, simply transfer it to a scale drawing, either on graph paper, where a square can represent a given distance, or on tracing paper laid over a similarly scaled grid.

The next stage is to rough in where the main features ought to go. Keep things of a kind together, such as dustbins, oil tank and log store; sheds, greenhouse and general maintenance gear; terrace, barbecue and built-in seating. Site these in relation to the general topography, so that sitting areas and vegetables are in sun, sheds and tanks are least obtrusive, sandpits and play space are in easy view of the house.

Link areas with paths that follow obvious 'desire lines' rather than with under-utilized serpentine meanders. Intervening areas will be taken up with paving, planting or lawn: the smaller the garden or yard, the simpler these shapes need to be.

As a general rule, areas close to the house should be 'architectural' to link with the building. Further away and around the perimeters they can be planned as a soft embracing backdrop that gives an impression of greater space.

Many of the thoughts painstakingly gathered during the survey and planning process may have to be rejected at some point. The usual problem is to find that not everything on a long list of requirements can possibly be accommodated. It is better to be realistic and cross the least important items from your list than it is to make an overly complicated plan.

Lastly, remember that designing is pattern-making and the simpler the pattern the more effective the end result.

So often modern gardens lack any real purpose and, while architects and interior designers produce schemes of real merit within a building, their ideas are far from practical when they move outside. This garden is quite different, and sets out to provide an environment not just for plants but for people too. The materials used are straightforward and underline the point that simplicity is paramount to any design. As a boundary, solid concrete block walls have been colour washed and capped with a neat brick coping. The line of the wall has been extended by crisp overhead beams that will, after a few years, be smothered in fragrant climbers and also provide light shade.

Planting is of course vital in what is an inherently architectural garden and the use of bold foliage and contrasting textures far outweighs brash colour. It is also interesting that many of these plants will provide a pattern throughout the year, rather than for a few months.

1 *City backyards can form a mosaic of often interlocking patterns which is invisible from the street. In many ways such gardens are not individual entities at all, but borrow trees and plants from one another until the whole centre of an urban block becomes a green and pleasant oasis.*

This tiny backyard illustrates the point perfectly, with ivy, roses and clematis smothering the boundaries and cascading into adjoining properties. Trees, too, are important, as they break the line of surrounding walls and often provide privacy from neighbouring windows. The combination of shade-casting trees and high walls in a limited space can make grass impractical. In this case, the problem is resolved by paving the garden in random rectangular slabs of York stone, which will last a lifetime.

A number of design factors can create interest, the most important being the change of level and the distribution of space. Here, the two go together, as the garden has been subdivided by planting with a simple step joining the two halves.

In design terms, this makes the whole composition far more interesting, particularly at ground level: one is directed through the space and not all is revealed at a single glance (see page 25). Garden furniture is agreeably simple and effective.

1

Before

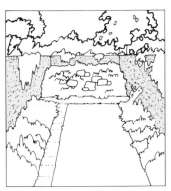

Before

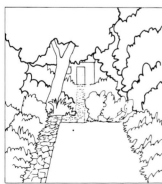

2   In this much larger garden, a lawn comes into its own. Don Drake, the designer, is an excellent plantsman, and what is more, he actually builds the gardens he designs himself, unlike most designers and landscape architects. Here, the soft green lawn flows like a river, sweeping away from the house in a series of delightfully fluid curves and providing continuity.

In many gardens this underlying design would lack strength of purpose, but the planting has been imaginatively planned and bold drifts tie the whole pattern together. The plants closest to the house, shown here in the foreground, are small and intimate, and the more distant areas are planted with larger species chosen for their handsome leaves and striking foliage.

'Tension points' are important design tools which guide both feet and eyes in a particular direction. The first of these is close to the house, between the pool and the planting; the second lies halfway up the garden and is dramatically highlighted by the brilliant drift of yellow alyssum.

The stepping stones in the strip of grass at the narrowest point of the garden reflect both practical and aesthetic considerations. Not only do they save wear on the turf, particularly in wet weather, but they are an added punctuation mark in the overall design.

1 *The simple fact of the matter is that not all garden design is good and, while this particular composition is acceptable, it could be much improved. When a garden is long and narrow the prime consideration, in all but a few specialized instances, is to subdivide that space into more manageable sections. All too often one sees a path down the middle, flanked by a washing line and planting in monotonous rectangular beds which only serve to emphasize the boundaries. This treatment exacerbates the problem.*

In this long, narrow garden, the path has at least been laid out off-centre, but the rigid ranks of vegetables in the patch to its left and the rectangular lawn to its right do little to soften or enliven the overall picture. A pool has been placed at the bottom of the garden in an obvious attempt to create a focal point – and it certainly does draw the eye. However, this is largely due to the soaring, spiky-leaved yucca in full flower behind it and the tall, cone-shaped conifers that act as punctuation marks.

The small stones that flank the lawn at the pool edge must be a continual nuisance when mowing the lawn.

By comparing this and the illustrations on the two previous pages you can see how different designs can radically alter the perspective of a garden.

1

2 *There is an unspoken rule in landscape design that 'less is more' and this garden illustrates the point perfectly. It is a simple setting in a contemporary mood with a timber-decked terrace adjoining the house. A change of level in this situation can often be awkward. Here a dry stream bed perfectly in harmony with the casual, naturalistic style of the house and deck has been created with boulders, washed gravel and planting.*
This garden also explodes the myth that gardens must be full of colour. The shades of green, the variegated leaves and the use of purple and black foliage add up to a controlled understatement.

3 *This delightful, unashamedly rural garden is in direct contrast to the distinctly urban gardens depicted elsewhere in this volume. Springtime gardens have a charm of their own. Here the pure white blossom of a flowering cherry tree underplanted with colourful tulips and hyacinths makes a perfect sitting area.*
The old stone wall provides stability, while the white deck chairs bring a feeling of freshness down to ground level. Spring grass is always greener and it is refreshing to see it left slightly longer. A closely mown lawn would look distinctly out of place.

1   *Whatever anyone says, first impressions count and this makes the treatment of a front garden particularly important. That first horticultural divide on entry to any domestic garden gives a very good idea of the owner's personality.*

The owner's personality is, however, only one facet and a front garden should take into account the character or style of the house, the possible inclusion of parking space and, of course, pedestrian access to the front or side doors. In other words, what is often a small space has to cater for a wide range of activities and requirements. Woven into and around fulfilment of the owner's requirements will be the distribution of plants and consideration of the inevitable impact on neighbours and the street scene as a whole. Whether it is formal or asymmetric, traditional or modern, the composition should above all be practical. This garden is one of ample size that has been developed as a little formal courtyard. The features are arranged symmetrically to balance the front elevation of the house, which has itself been softened by clematis and honeysuckle.

2

3

4

5

2 *Timber cladding and bright walls frame a collection of herbs that carry around the corner of the house to the steps. The sensibly broad path is edged in brick, which always forms an ideal backdrop for warm terracotta pots, and the theme is echoed by the course of brickwork on top of the wall.*

3 *Gravel is a no-nonsense, low-maintenance ground cover, ideal for an urban situation. Its 'fluid' nature enables it to conform to any awkward shape, in this case the pattern set up by the bay window. Planting can also be allowed to grow through gravel, so there is no real need for a formal bed. The troughs on the window sills add colour.*

4 *With a small space, and particularly when an immediate impression is important, it can be vital for a design to turn in upon itself. This symmetrical pattern centres on an octagonal bed planted with spring-flowering daffodils. Later this could be changed to summer bedding plants or a permanent display of shrubs.*

5 *A well-planted garden path is always inviting. The charm of this green entryway embraces even the gateposts at the entrance, which are in need of attention. Broad-leaved hosta, bergenia and euonymus all spill out to soften the line.*

The drawings on this page and those following illustrate, step by step, the stages involved in coming to grips with a design for any garden, from surveying the existing garden, to making a conceptual sketch plan for the new one, to working out a detailed plan for hard landscaping and planting. Before starting your survey, make a list of everything you might want from your garden. If you have moved house, take a full year to see what plants appear from season to season and to learn which parts of the garden receive sun and shade at different times of the year. Then go out into the garden with a long measuring tape, paper and pencil and make a rough survey of the existing garden. Draw a plan of the site, indicating the house (with windows and doors marked). Be sure to note down all relevant items: changes of level, the north point, bad views to be screened, good views to be enhanced and the location of existing features, such as plants, trees, other buildings, fences and so forth. Take running measurements of important distances.

The survey drawing of this sample garden reveals a large central lawn bisected by a clothesline with features clustered along two boundaries. There are some features worth retaining, such as the trees, shed and roses.

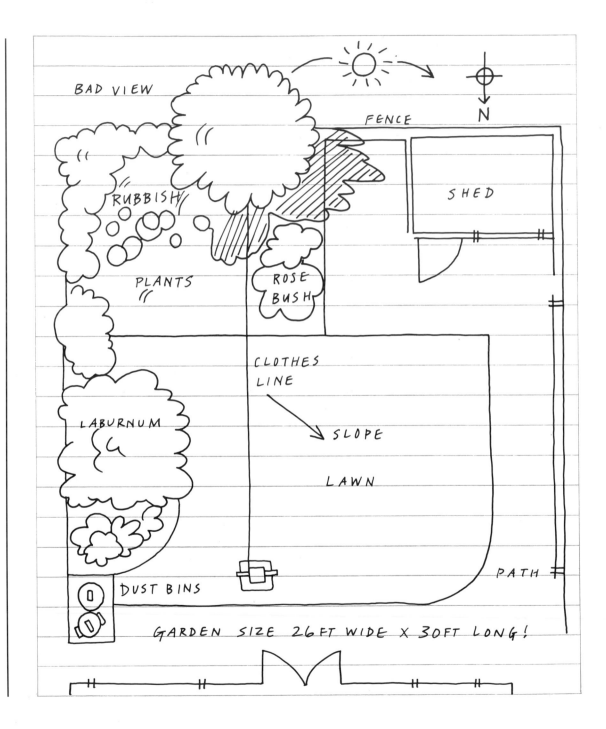

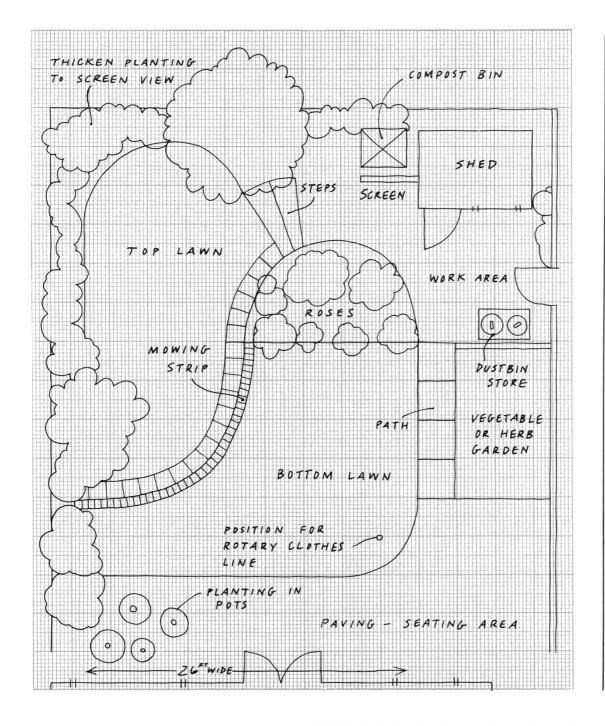

THICKEN PLANTING
TO SCREEN VIEW

COMPOST BIN

SHED

STEPS

SCREEN

TOP LAWN

WORK AREA

ROSES

MOWING
STRIP

DUSTBIN
STORE

PATH

VEGETABLE
OR HERB
GARDEN

BOTTOM LAWN

POSITION FOR
ROTARY CLOTHES
LINE

PLANTING IN
POTS

PAVING — SEATING AREA

26 FT WIDE

Once you have measured and mapped existing features on a rough survey drawing, transfer the information you have gathered to a scale drawing, using the running measurements to plot accurately those existing features you wish to keep or change. Some prefer to do this using gridded paper, where each square represents a unit of measurement (1m or 1ft). With your list of garden requirements and survey drawing you are ready to start designing the new one. Begin with your list of requirements, numbering each item in order of priority. Work through the list, marking the area to be allocated to each function on a copy of the scale drawing, giving the most space to those features which you consider most important. It will be handy at this stage to have several copies of your scale drawings, since even experienced garden designers make several conceptual sketch plans as their ideas develop. Especially in a small garden or backyard, it is important to think carefully about the location of each feature and to try and draw related elements together. The challenge posed by the small backyard illustrated here is to give the eventual design a real feeling of space and movement which is lacking in the original.

The finished plan of the sample garden reveals ample room for a sitting/dining area, and for a small food garden with espalier fruit trees. Dustbins, which previously were an inconveniently located eyesore, occupy the space beyond near the gate and are concealed by a screen smothered in evergreen ivy. There is space for a work area near the original shed, with a compost heap next to it also screened by a climbing plant. The sloping lawn has been rationalized by creating two lawns on different levels divided by a path and a neat 'mowing strip'. The main lawn and border shapes are built up from strong, flowing curves, giving a sense of continuity. When the basic framework of the garden has been established, it can be useful to make sketches of the elevation of those areas where planting is required in order to help visualize the final effect (see opposite). Here, maximum use has been made of walls and fences for climbing plants. Fast-growing bamboo (Arundinaria nitida) screens the bad view from the far corner, and other planting has been chosen to provide colour and foliage year round. Even in winter, the red stems of the dogwood (Cornus alba) at the bottom add interest. There is plenty of room for adding spring-flowering bulbs and summer-flowering annuals.

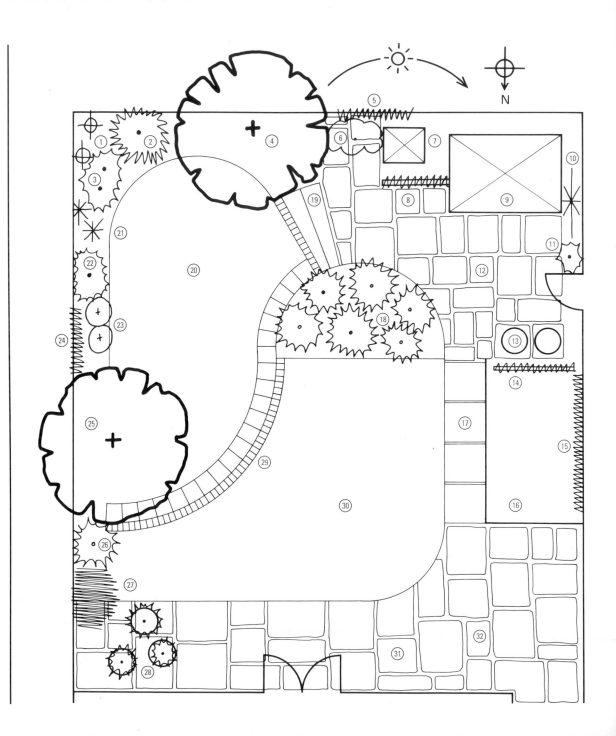

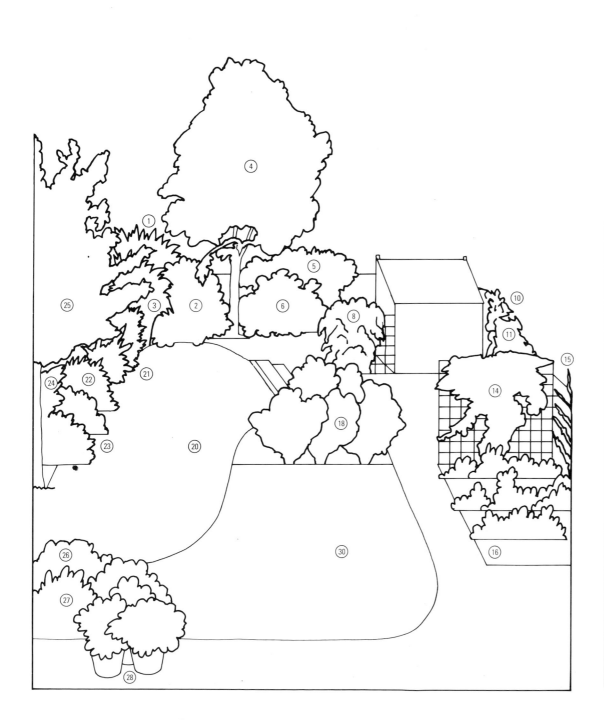

1 *Two* Arundinaria nitida
2 Cornus alba *'Elegantissima'*
3 *Two* Weigela *'Bristol Ruby'*
4 *Existing birch tree*
5 Clematis montana *growing on fence*
6 Hydrangea *'New Wave'*
7 *Compost heap*
8 *Screen for compost heap with* Jasminum nudiflorum *growing on it*
9 *Existing shed*
10 Hydrangea petiolaris *growing on fence*
11 Kerria japonica
12 *Random paving*
13 *Dustbins*
14 *Screen for dustbins with ivy growing on it*
15 *Espalier fruit trees growing on wall*
16 *Vegetable and herb garden*
17 *Steps*
18 *Floribunda roses*
19 *Curved steps*
20 *Upper lawn*
21 *Two* Mahonia japonica
22 Buddleia *'Black Knight'*
23 *Two* Spiraea *'Anthony Waterer'*
24 Lonicera periclymenum *'Belgica' and 'Serotina' growing on wall*
25 Existing laburnum tree
26 Cytisus kewiensis
27 Potentilla *'Katherine Dykes'*
28 *Flowering annuals in pots*
29 *Brick mowing edge*
30 *Lower lawn*
31 *Random paving*
32 *Seating/dining area*

1 *Brick building, brick walls, brick floor – all in harmony and small enough in scale not to become oppressive. Simple steps lead up from a basement flat with plants growing on every possible square inch, including the walls. Terracotta containers of different shapes and sizes associate well with the brickwork. The flimsy plastic trellis, however, breaks the line of the wall. A discreet horizontal wire, fixed unobtrusively with nails or vine-eyes, would have been a better choice of support for the climbing plant.*

2 *This tiny backyard is completely surrounded by walls, and the feeling of enclosure is heightened by the use of overhead beams to support light-loving climbing plants. Surfaces have been painted white to reflect maximum light. Even so, only shade-tolerant plants will thrive in such a sheltered spot. Statuary adds personality and year-round interest.*

3 *This splendid little garden gets away with breaking the rule of simplicity. There is so much going on that it really should not work well at all. However, rules are there to be broken. Most designers would have kept to a single paving material, but the central panel of slabs is strong enough to be positive and it acts as a host to the fine range of pots.*

1

2

3

4   Roof gardens are quite literally in a world of their own. More often than not they are created despite the hostile roof environment with its unique microclimate of high winds and lack of shelter. But roofs are often the only space available to urban gardeners and this makes the effort they require worthwhile.
The load-bearing potential of a roof and the question of shelter are so important that professional advice is vital. In this garden, both factors have been catered for with an opaque glass screen and lightweight asbestos tiles. The lush planting is entirely in containers and provides a successful alternative to the surrounding roofscape.

5   Trompe-l'oeil *painting employs perspective and delicate shading to deceive the eye and create an illusion of space. The trompe-l'oeil* wall of this enclosed garden, much like more common indoor *trompe-l'oeil* painting, is used to create an architectural interest which is lacking. This is not to everyone's taste: a more horticultural approach to such a wall would be to smother it with plants.

6   This is the tiny backyard garden shown on page 14 as it looks at ground level. It illustrates just how much a different viewpoint can alter one's perception of a well-designed garden.

1   *Much of garden design is about surprise. In a small area this often means creating discreet areas with dividers so that the observer is drawn by curiosity from one space to another. In this garden a clematis-covered screen and arch act as wall and doorway framing a view of the raised pool which is set as a focal point within the composition as a whole. The planting is cool, casual and undemonstrative, the fountain simple yet effective, with the pool surround doubling as an occasional seat.*

2   *Two materials infrequently used in Britain are exposed aggregate concrete and timber decking, which is a pity as both have attractive characteristics. Here concrete cylinders of different heights set in a staggered pattern form steps up to the deck, an imaginative solution to a common problem in garden design. Small-scale ground-level circular paving continues the theme and plants act as a foil to the architectural composition.*

3   *This English garden has a distinctly informal Mediterranean feel. The architect owner designed the sensitive grouping of plants and the use of the marvellous pot as sculpture. It often makes sense to resist the temptation to cram every container full of foliage.*

4 *Slate may be expensive, but in gardening, possibly more than anywhere else, you get what you pay for. This superb slate surface acts as a perfect foil for planting and sets up the most fascinating reflections, even when dry. The loose cobbles are an attractive contrast, leading the eye away to the timber-decked terrace.*

5 *A formal and elegant simplicity is achieved by setting a sculptural glazed pot against a background of natural stone paving. At poolside, the paving slabs overhang the water and create a clean, sharp, dark line of shadow. The important balance between 'hard' and 'soft' landscape is handled sensitively in this garden, preventing either element from becoming dominant.*

6 *Here, two outdoor rooms are divided by a fine old brick wall clothed in rampant rambling roses. The archway highlights the transition from one to the other, as does the band of shade it casts between the sunlit areas.*

7 *It is difficult to create an authentic Japanese garden outside Japan, but a suggestion is always possible. Here, chippings, stepping stones, a lantern and the bold-leaved lungwort combine to form an attractive little Japanese-style composition.*

1 *This extraordinarily attractive frontyard is an excellent example of how to extend living space outside. The long roof frames a wall of sliding glass doors which open on to and reflect the bold, simple and imaginative planting. Otherwise, paving and soft landscaping have been kept to a minimum. The result is a perfectly understated setting for an outdoor meal.*

2 *This impeccably handled front approach sets the building off beautifully. The grading and juxtaposition of the plants, from the overhanging robinia right down to the ground-hugging species, is particularly effective. The use of warm, terracotta tiles provides intimacy and overall continuity.*

3 *Built-in seating is both attractive and practical. In a small garden it also saves space. Here, a change of level has been particularly well handled, with plants softening the line of the retaining walls. Raised beds make it easier to observe small plants.*

4 *Here the thin slats of built-in timber seating draw the eye and then turn across the garden to form a step. In this clever design the steps themselves are well detailed; both they and the retaining walls are softened by planting.*

5

5 Paving and planting are truly vital, basic garden ingredients and they are combined here to form a superb arrangement. This seemingly haphazard arrangement did not just 'happen', but was very, very carefully planned, with great attention to detail and the placement of plants and furniture. This spot serves both as a sitting area and as a pathway out into the garden beyond. The designer has used his limited space imaginatively, creating a soft and intimate alcove for the assortment of seats, table and chairs.

In direct contrast to the small-scale brick paving, the planting relies heavily on the sculptural use of foliage rather than brash flower colour. The giant leaves of Gunnera manicata associate particularly well with the adjoining hosta and the nearby bronze-leaved Japanese maple. Even after these latter two deciduous plants have lost their summer foliage, there is sufficient evergreen material here to provide winter interest as well.

Many people find it difficult to place statues, sculpture or other objects of intrinsic interest in a garden. They should have a positive position and should not be dumped down anywhere. As focal points in and of themselves, they often look well with handsome foliage, as the bust does here.

The paving, walling and hard surfacing of a garden really provide the basic structure of any composition. They also account for roughly seventy-five per cent of the total garden budget.

In design terms, the problem with hard surfaces is largely one of choice as the market is flooded with a wealth of materials, natural and artificial, all with widely differing properties, design characteristics, availability and prices.

The best way out of this particular maze is once again to think of paving in terms of flooring. Very few people would think of mixing their internal floor coverings, but how many times do you see elaborate, hideous amalgamations of paving that are as hard on the eye as they are on the pocketbook?

In fact paving, whether it be in the form of terraces, paths, drives or hardstanding areas, should have a unifying influence, providing a sensible, low-key background for the wealth of activities proper to a small garden, from barbecuing to babysitting.

To a large extent this applies to walling as well, where there is in addition a greater responsibility to respect local traditions and the surrounding environment. The practicality of extending a brick wall from a brick building should be obvious in both visual and financial terms. Not only are the materials compatible but they will almost certainly be available locally. It would be foolish to import natural stone over vast distances in such a case. Planning in terms of the existing built environment can leave you with a more manageable shortlist of acceptable options.

For those lucky enough to have a stone, brick or slate floor indoors, the treatment of an adjoining paved area is ready-made. When reinforced by planting, continuity of paving will form the ultimate link between inside and out.

Simplicity is once again the key to these areas, so only a few materials should be used within a design. If a single surface, perhaps of brick or slabs, could become visually heavy, it can make sense to mix materials. In a traditional setting, random rectangular stone flags could be interspersed with panels of brick. In a contemporary design, crisp brick courses could run out from a building to form a grid which is then filled in with neatly pointed precast slabs.

Some materials, such as gravel, concrete and tarmac, are 'fluid' and can be cast or laid to a free-flowing pattern, which is ideal for a drive or broad winding path where larger individual modules would need cutting to shape. This also applies to small-scale materials such as cobbles or granite paving stones.

Finally, choose and use your hard landscape materials sensibly: they are expensive, and they will last a lifetime. They form the basic framework of your garden, to be decorated to your taste with plants and furnishings, but changed only with difficulty.

There are a number of unusual things about this composition, not the least of which is that it works so well. Drama is an essential design tool, but only effective if used sparingly. Sculpture can take many forms and need not necessarily be a single subject. This small corner of what is undoubtedly a far grander lay-out forms a unified sculptural group. The dramatic herringbone brick path gives a focus to the equally bold stone seat. The latter is probably eighteenth century and there is no doubt that age, which is obvious here, has a charisma of its own. The gryphon armrests are a sort of latter-day 'gnomery', amusing in their own right and simply hinting at the grander architectural style used elsewhere in the garden. The hedge is of pleached lime trees, a device that can be used to good effect in both large and small gardens. It is all the more telling here for being left slightly ragged, as it heightens the drama below. The real point is that this is 'landscape architecture' in the fullest sense.

1 *Garden structure can be classified into two broad categories: hard and soft landscape. The proportion of one or the other is largely determined by the pattern of use – pedestrian traffic or seating mean hard landscaping, plants and lawns mean soft. In reality there is usually a pretty even split. Whereas plants may look satisfactory with only a modicum of care, provided that their soil and situation are suitable, paving can look a total disaster if incorrectly or poorly laid. Attention spent on hard landscape work is therefore essential, not only because of its high cost but also because it can last a lifetime.*

This particular composition is strongly architectural; the line of steps and paving link positively with the strong lines of the house. Indeed, the very materials of the hard landscaping complement and echo those of the building with its prominent roof. Steps radiate from pivot points established by the raised beds. Each riser of the steps is formed by sawn-down sleepers, and plants soften the natural flight.

It is a common myth that trees planted close to a building are naturally destructive. Some species, such as willow and poplar, should certainly be avoided, but less rampant varieties are acceptable.

2

3

HOW TO LAY PAVING

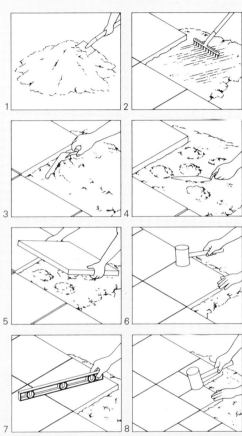

1   2

3   4

5   6

7   8

Where paving slabs meet up with buildings, paving surfaces must be at least 155mm (6in) below any damp course.

1 Mix sand and cement with a shovel until the colour of the mixture is even throughout. **2** Lay a thin bed of sand for each paving slab and rake it smooth. **3** Use a trowel to scrape any excess sand to ensure that there is a clean edge between paving slabs. **4** Make five small mounds of sand for each slab. **5** Ease each paving slab carefully and gently into position. **6** Gently firm the slabs in place using a mallet. **7** Check with a spirit level to ensure that paving slabs slope away from the house. **8** Small paving slabs may be laid directly on to a bed of sand unmixed with cement.

2 *Not all paving is tasteful and the pink stepping stones across this pool are distinctly dubious. Coloured slabs are visually dangerous: they fade to pallid tints and tend to clash with furniture, plants and virtually everything else. In this case, it would have been better to continue the line of paving in the neutral buff colour. Colour control is also less than perfect with the planting. The variegated hosta vies uncomfortably with the fiercely pink azalea blossom. The terracotta pot contains a diversity of material lacking cohesion, and its position is arbitrary. It is far too easy to slap a pot down anywhere: rather use them like sculpture, either singly or in well-positioned groups.*

3 *This immensely effective design demonstrates what a versatile material timber can be in the hands of an imaginative designer. Sleepers have been used to form steps, while solid balks of wood act as a retainer to the raised bed flanking the flight on the left. By varying the height of these uprights the designer has set up a rhythm that echoes the flight itself. The planting is refreshingly simple and naturalistic. Over-zealous weeding between the slabs would destroy the charm of the design.*

1 In this crisp Mediterranean setting, tiles form an ideal link between inside and out. In colder climates, care must be taken to ensure that such tiles are frost-proof, as many will not stand a severe winter. Porches or verandahs are ideal in hot weather, allowing a cool circulation of air and a gentle transition from the house into the garden.

2 This patio is a scaled-up version of a far-from-restful Victorian tiled floor. Bright colours are appropriate here and the cheerful tulips are particularly effective.

3 For many years clay bricks were one of the few small-scale paving materials available. Although attractive, they could be damaged relatively easily, particularly by frost. Recently a number of manufacturers have started producing concrete paving slabs that can be quickly and easily laid on a bed of sand. They have chamfered edges and can be butt-jointed, eliminating pointing.

4 Lightweight tiles are often essential for a roof garden and these asbestos squares are commonly used. They provide a neat, straightforward, no-nonsense background for furniture and planting.

5 Hard bricks are still an excellent choice and are laid here in a traditional 'basketweave' pattern. The pattern, or bond as it is more correctly called, has considerable visual impetus. If a path or terrace is laid in bricks positioned end to end, this will lead the eye on. Herringbone laid across the line is more static.

6 These are very hard pavers, completely frost-proof and capable of withstanding a life-time's wear. They have been laid in a random pattern in this tiny backyard, forming a practical path to the back door and an attractive foil to the white-painted house. As they run into the planting, the edge of the path need not be cut to form a rigid line.

7   This timber deck visually echoes the broad boards of the fence and the section in the foreground of the picture is carefully varied with uneven widths. The planting is restrained and the furniture simple. How pleasant to step out from those sliding doors!

8   Log slices can make very attractive informal stepping stones through a lawn, planting or, as in this case, gravel. The type of timber is important and any of the hardwoods is ideal. If this treatment is used across a lawn, be sure to set the slices below the turf to prevent difficulty when mowing.

9   Cobbles are a traditional paving and have been used for many thousands of years. While they have been superseded for most roads and footways owing to their irregular nature, they still form an attractive small-scale surface. The municipal habit of laying them like currants in a bun should be avoided at all costs. They should be packed tightly together like eggs in a crate.

10   Granite paving stones, or setts, are another traditional material originally used for street paving. In Britain, they can still be obtained from demolition contractors or council yards and are extremely hard. Their slightly uneven nature makes them unsuitable under tables and chairs, but for drives and paths they provide an ideal non-slip surface.

11   Brick paving, another traditional material, is here laid in soldier courses which lead the eye towards the sundial. Shallow steps, however, can be a little awkward. An ideal height for a garden step is 15cm (6in), or two bricks deep.

12   John Brookes is another talented designer and this was his own garden in London. It provides a perfect invitation outside and is virtually maintenance free. The simple gravel floor blends well with the surrounding brickwork.

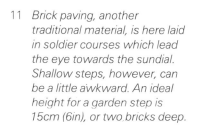

1 Fencing is one of the most expensive jobs in the garden, and often one of the most poorly designed features. The problem is, of course, that there is a lack of really attractive fencing available and most people think solely in terms of closeboard or interwoven panels. In reality, the choice is far wider than this. Any fencing should be selected with respect for its surroundings, including both the owner's home and garden and the neighbours' scheme. Although timber is the natural choice, fences are also made in wire and plastic. Wire fencing is generally chosen when security is important, both to keep pets in and unwelcome visitors out. It is not practical for screening a view or acting as a wind-break, but could have its uses where a glimpse of landscape would be pleasant.

Plastic fencing can be appalling. If used properly, taking account of its inherent versatility, it can also look superb.

The fence illustrated here is made from simple vertical timber slats, spaced with a slight gap between each. It is handsome, relatively inexpensive and an ideal foil for planting. It is also worth remembering that a 'permeable' screen, such as this, tends to filter the wind, causing far less turbulence than a solid barrier.

1

TYPES OF FENCING

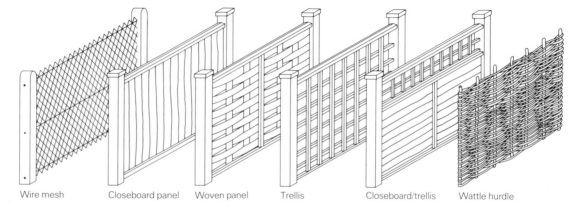

Wire mesh   Closeboard panel   Woven panel   Trellis   Closeboard/trellis   Wattle hurdle

2

2 *Beehive, roses and salad greens are here mixed together in a traditional setting. The fine osier hurdles in the background are woven from willow stems and were originally designed for penning sheep. They are a little more expensive than conventional fence panels, but are easy to erect as they are simply wired to round posts driven into the ground. Their life expectancy of eight to ten years is quite respectable, often ideal while a developing border or hedge takes hold. They are a wonderful foil for planting and in such a position form an elegant backdrop. Here, they provide a contrast to the striking white beehive. Other woven fences include wattle hurdles, which are made from strips of hazel, and also reed fences which use bundles of reeds bound in panels. The path in this garden is equally attractive, the herringbone brick being well laid and retained by neat soldier courses on either side. Maintenance of fences is important too and a coat of non-toxic (never creosote) preservative should be applied every two years. In order to prevent rotting at the bottom, fit a gravel board nailed or screwed to the posts. This can be replaced when necessary without renewing the panels. Finally, support climbing plants on wires stretched between the posts.*

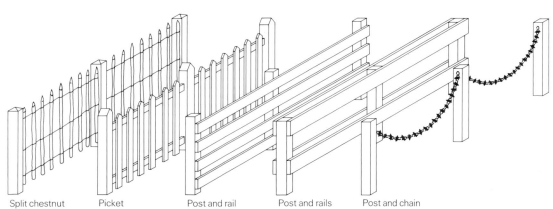

Split chestnut   Picket   Post and rail   Post and rails   Post and chain

1 *This is an altogether charming garden, somewhat unkempt and almost entirely natural. This belies careful planning and reinforces one of the basic rules that a garden should remain architectural close to a building, but merge into a softer, looser composition further away. By doing this one can create a far greater feeling of space.*

One of the secrets of informal steps is that the ends of the treads can merge into the planting on either side. There is no need for a rigid flight – in fact, the pattern can be staggered from side to side so that one step offsets the next. In many ways the materials are unimportant. Whether the steps are composed from timber, slabs or brick, it is the character of this garden that really matters.

These are in fact railway sleepers, ideal for the purpose and virtually indestructible. They can be simply bedded in position on a minimal foundation of well-compacted soil, although two wedges, one on either side, will ensure there is no movement, especially after wet or frosty weather. As far as the planting is concerned, poppies and wild flowers are here far more effective than 'architectural' shrubs. It underlines the point that species have unique and individual characters.

1

2

3

2   *Landscape architecture, a multidisciplinary blend of building and horticultural design, can be practised on an infinite number of scales. It presupposes that architecture and landscape are complementary. Although small in scale, these steps perfectly illustrate the art. Here, brick steps run directly off a building. The junction between them and the white wall is enlivened by a sprawling mat of Mexican wall daisies (Erigeron mucronatus). Bricks turned on edge are almost the ideal height for the riser of a step, but it is particularly important to use a hard, well-fired variety of brick that will be frost resistant. Engineering bricks, although very durable, are often glazed and can become slippery when wet, so they are best avoided.*

3   *The concept behind this garden is clever, but the construction of the steps is not. The levels are slightly wrong and the treads run at awkward angles. In theory, L-shaped steps can be very attractive and the more space there is available for them the better. There should be ample room for pots and plants, as here. In this case, the positioning of the flight to one side of the garden is more effective than it would have been right in the middle. The planting is pretty and the overall setting attractive, but the steps could be better.*

1   *In this gentle garden with muted colours, the low hedge allows one's view to run out to the more distant parts of the composition, creating a feeling of space and an element of surprise. The arch framing the pathway does more than just support climbing plants: it invites the visitor in positive terms to walk under or through to the next area. Space division is one of the garden designer's most useful tools. It creates a feeling of mystery, adds depth to a composition and provides endless scope for surprise. Such internal separations can be achieved by a variety of means – from walling, through fences and screens, down to hedges – and the height of all of these can be varied.*

2   *This is another arch in a quite different situation. This really is full of promise. A curved path always gives a hint of the unexpected, and this one is most evocative. The series of arches establishes a rhythm that carries the eye onward. Wire or iron arches cause minimal visual disruption and allow any climbing plants visual success. These arches are perfectly built and their shape echoes that of the old brick path. Pale yellow climbing roses link with the lady's mantle (Alchemilla mollis) at ground level, while trees form a canopy at a higher level.*

3 *Where the two gardens on the opposite page are distinctly informal, these rigid, neatly clipped hedges take on a more controlled presence. While one can see over them when standing, the sight-line is broken when sitting down. This is another fundamental consideration in garden design and opens up a number of interesting possibilities.*
The brick paving and low walls mimic the line of the hedge and are precisely positioned to match the end of the run in the middle distance. The steps provide a transition between two levels, and this garden provides the perfect vehicle for developing separate themes or colours in different sections.
A number of famous English gardens do just this: Hidcote Manor in Gloucestershire and Sissinghurst in Kent are perhaps the most famous. Such subdivision not only allows diversity within an overall garden concept but also increases the feeling of space. Sissinghurst is surprisingly small when seen from the tower, but has an enormous amount of rich detail when seen at ground level. Continuity, however, is important and this can be achieved in a number of ways. The dividing walls or hedges can be of a type and so too can the paving. These will act as a framework against which more complicated themes can be allowed free rein.

If we continue to think of the backyard as simply another room adjoining the home, then furnishing that space is vitally important. The size of the garden poses certain limitations, but surprising results can be achieved in a very limited space, especially using pots, containers, hanging baskets and window boxes. One very famous balcony garden set in the heart of London is suspended many hundreds of feet above the city. In this tiny and unlikely area the gifted owner has created a paradise of plants fitted into every conceivable corner. Many of the containers have been recycled from other uses, but once smothered in foliage no one knows the difference.

Conversely, the most unexpected and successful compositions can often be achieved by featuring unlikely objects as plant containers. For example, a delightful Alpine garden can be created in a bath tub filled with rubble and topped with sharp-draining soil. The plug hole allows excess water to escape and the whole composition can be most effective, almost a self-contained miniature landscape.

Water has a charm all its own and in a small urban garden it can make all the difference on an overpoweringly hot summer day by transforming a stuffy courtyard into a refreshing oasis. Scale is of course vital – there is little point in building a vast pool to house a large fountain in a tiny courtyard. It is perhaps the sound of water that is most important, the splashing of a bubble jet or a simple slide that sends a cascade into a pool below.

In many situations a pool of standing water is not necessary at all and a millstone or boulder can be drilled to accept a pipe. The whole arrangement can then be positioned over a water tank, let into the ground or a raised bed, and a submersible pump installed to recirculate water continuously around the system.

Furniture is another area where people's ideas tend to dry up when they move outside, although careful shopping for garden furniture and other features is worth the effort. The range of items from which to choose is enormous: tables, chairs, trolleys, lounge chairs, parasols, garden benches, swings and more are made in a wide variety of styles. Remember that painted finishes will soon become shabby with exposure to the elements and that you must be prepared for frequent repainting if you opt for painted metal or timber furniture.

In a small space it makes sense to build in seating, and in so doing it is often possible to produce a continuity that pulls the design together. Raised beds and broad walls at the right height are always inviting, while overhead beams or arbours can define a sitting area, casting welcome shade.

As with hard and soft landscape, keep furnishings to a theme. The odd, well-chosen piece or feature can certainly act as a contrast, but let it work against a sensible rather than discordant background.

A conservatory is a hybrid, halfway between house and garden. Its original function in historical terms was as a glorified greenhouse, in which plants were grown specifically for use in the adjoining house. In the nineteenth century all this changed and, with the greater facility for the production of glass and wrought iron, a superb range of buildings arrived.

Some of these remain today and there are also a number of excellent reproductions that are worthy of the name. The function of such a building is to form a transition. A conservatory can be enormously attractive. As a sitting room it is delightful, particularly on those winter or spring days that look inviting enough to sit outside but are really just too cold. They also extend the range of plant material that can be grown. The setting in this garden room is softened by a sensitive planting scheme and paved with old York stone, reinforcing the traditional setting.

1 *People always confuse pergolas, arbours, gazebos and pavilions. The last two are buildings; the first, a series of arches framing a path; while an arbour is a place in which to sit. All these structures are subject to a form of gardening snobbery which considers it advantageous to boast some sort of feature, no matter how far removed it may be from the original concept.*

The arbour illustrated here is of the very best kind. It is a pretty little structure, with fine old cast-iron columns and a soaring, peaked lattice-work roof that is smothered in climbing plants. White paintwork is traditional for a structure of this sort, although painted finishes are not always practical, as they can become drab in a short period.

Potted plants are arranged on a series of white wire racks, an unusual but attractive idea. The curved seat continues the theme of white metalwork, but the blue tablecloth and patterned cushions introduce a welcome colour break, preventing the composition from becoming bland. Fragrance is an essential ingredient of such an idyllic setting: honeysuckle (Lonicera) is always a favourite climbing plant, though summer-flowering jasmine (Jasminum officinale) or roses would be equally good.

2 Good design is timeless and is to do with proportion, form and balance. This garden illustrates all these qualities and features built-in furniture as an integral part of the design. It is composed of a number of elements, but notice how the simple fence has been lined up exactly with the concrete-block wall. The raised pool is attractive, while the timber seat cleverly runs around the right angles, drawing the whole composition together.

3 In this pretty little garden an old hand pump has been used to create an unusual feature. Water is recirculated from the pool below using a submersible electric pump. The sound of playing water gives this garden its greatest inherent charm. The planting is both delicate and successful, using a combination of waterside species, climbing plants and herbs. The background fence is constructed from osier hurdles.

4 Running water can feature even in a garden lacking a pool. Here an old millstone has been drilled to accept a pipe. The whole arrangement has been positioned over a water tank and water is pumped through the stone to fall back into the tank on a recirculating basis. The arrangement of loose cobbles, planting, gravel and brick is unusual, but effective.

1   Humour can be an integral part of any garden which reflects its owner's personality and individual taste. Sculpture, and the use of interesting objects in sculptural ways, is a time-tested way of adding unique interest, whether it be a garden gnome, perhaps a little red-capped fellow leaning on a rake — an example of much-maligned but classic English garden kitsch — or a sculpture by Henry Moore. Here, planting plays second fiddle to this quite delightful group of pots.

2   This sophisticated garden underlines the point that it is often the planting rather than the container that is important. The pot could be any container — a bucket or a priceless vase — it simply does not matter. The colour combination of pink pelargonium, blue lobelia and grey helichrysum is charming and works well against the architectural garage doors behind. The cobbles are also superbly laid.

3   The strong primary colours of these gay pots are reminiscent of the signwriting and painting so often found on English canal narrowboats and barges. Far from being irrelevant to the overall effect, these pots fight for attention with their bright colours, and it is right to plant them with something undemonstrative — bright flowers in this case would ruin the effect.

4 *Seats and pots are two vital garden furnishings and are often sited with little regard to their own intrinsic character or the overall garden pattern. Here, the siting is quite superb: the old iron seat nestles comfortably below the wisteria. The half-barrel is host to sprawling agapanthus and helps to bring the eye down to a lower level. In this case, the choice of simple hard landscape materials and design is a happy one.*

5 *Water gardens in containers are not always easy to maintain, as plants can often quickly outstrip their allotted space. There is also a problem with the oxygen balance — perhaps we should say imbalance — and such small areas can turn green very quickly. However, if tended regularly they can be both attractive and practical, as this old half-barrel shows. The timber edging for the raised beds is made from sawn logs set in concrete. To be really successful, the planting should be more generous, spilling over and softening the outline.*

6 *The colour and planting of these bowls is excellent, while the setting is eminently suitable. Such groups are sculpture in their own right and it would be quite wrong to straighten up the right-hand pot, as some over-zealous gardeners might do.*

PLANTING

Once the structure of the hard landscape is in position we can move into the third dimension with planting.

To many people this is really what gardening is all about and there is no doubt that plants, trees and shrubs bring a carefully planned design to life. But where there were a few pitfalls to avoid and sound rules to obey when planning the lay-out, there are even more when considering planting design.

Any oak woodland, one of Britain's richest natural habitats, has a definite vertical stratum of vegetation. The trees themselves form the highest canopy, under which occurs a shrub layer that in turn overshadows a layer of low ground-covering plants. This pattern should be echoed in the garden with a progression of elements from the highest tree that provides vertical emphasis, right down to carpeting species that reduce maintenance to a sensible minimum.

The way in which such a composition is built up can follow a planned sequence. Trees come first and should be sited with regard to screening, the creation of shade and their general large-scale impact on the design as a whole.

Shrubs come next, and here a framework of taller, often evergreen plants provides shelter and protection. Faster-growing species which can be removed once surrounding plants have reached maturity are often useful at first.

With this framework in place, fill in with lighter, more colourful plants, such as smaller shrubs, herbaceous perennials, bulbs and areas for annuals and containers.

Over-complicated planting schemes are the curse of many gardens. As a general rule use drifts of material, allowing these to lead the eye through the curve or around a corner.

Colour, too, is vital but here again there are sensible rules that engender harmony. Hot, vibrant colours such as orange, red and yellow draw the eye and foreshorten a space, so keep them close to the house or viewpoint for maximum effect. This will allow the cooler range of blue, purple, pink and white to run on to the boundaries, creating a feeling of greater space. Grey, possibly the designer's most useful colour, is a harmonizer, useful as a softening influence and a vital link between more demonstrative colours.

PLANTING CHECKLIST

- Have you carried out an accurate survey and prepared a scale plan? (See Garden Planning Checklist, page 5.)
- What existing plants, trees or shrubs do you wish to keep?
- Are you bringing plants from elsewhere – if so, what?
- Do you have any favourite plants or particular dislikes?
- What type of soil do you have? Sandy, clay, loam, acid or chalky?
- How much sunshine do different areas get, and for how long?
- What are the prevailing weather conditions? Rainfall? Temperature?
- How long will you stay at this house? Short-term, medium-term or long-term?
- What is your budget for plants?
- Do you wish to exclude all poisonous plants?
- What are the colour schemes of the rooms adjoining or overlooking the garden?
- Do you have any colour preferences?
- Do you want year-round interest, or seasonal emphasis at a particular time of year?

In most respects plants are a garden. It is their form, colour, texture and size that breathe life into a composition. To be successful there should be a balance of species. Because of its predominance of summer-flowering herbaceous plants, this garden is at its best from June to August.

1 *Plants can conjure up any mood, from crisp and architectural to flagrantly rural, as here. This classic English cottage garden mixes an assortment of shrubs, perennials and annuals. The daisied lawn and slightly ragged bushes express the owner's respect for natural-looking forms and plants.*

2 *Conifers, if properly used, can provide enormous interest at times of year when other species are not at their best. This arrangement emphasizes the point that they are most impressive in a group, where differences in colour and texture can be appreciated. Be careful to learn what the ultimate size of any conifer will be.*

3 *Pink, purple and grey is a classic colour combination in almost any design situation, especially in a garden. Clematis is a climbing plant which blossoms abundantly.* Helichrysum angustifolium *and* Lamium maculatum *complete the colour scheme close to the ground.*

4 *Good design often looks uncontrived, as here, where a simple seat echoes the solid line of the railway sleepers that edge the lawn. It also 'ties' together the two wings of planting, with lady's mantle* (Alchemilla mollis) *acting as a carpet.*

5

5 *This garden has all the hallmarks of a successful composition. Hostas are another essential plant for any garden; their broad leaves and distinctive colouring act as a foil in any situation. Their foliage ranges from the bold glaucous leaves of* Hosta sieboldiana, *illustrated here, through the variegated types, of which the green and white striped variety 'Thomas Hogg' is perhaps the best, to those with undulating and even yellow foliage. Hostas tolerate both sun and shade and are a 'must' for flower arranging. Here, delphinium makes an unusual but effective partner and the tall spike of dark blue does much to 'lift' this corner. Perhaps the most intriguing component of this design is the old wall with its open door, which affords a tantalizing glimpse of an altogether wider, sunlit landscape, illustrating once again the vital role played by surprise in garden design. Here, the drama is heightened by the transition between shadow and light. This is a technique used most often in hot climates, but it can be used to good effect in more temperate zones as well, where shadows cast by walls and trees can add interest and depth to a situation.*
The brick path serves the practical function of simplifying maintenance and protecting flower and foliage from the blades of a lawnmower.

1   *The area at the side of a house, generally little more than a long, narrow thoroughfare with little room to spare, is often a problem. More often than not it gets forgotten or becomes a storage area for hiding away all those unsightly odds and ends that accumulate in any garden. Here the approach has been altogether different and a sensitive planting plan has been carried out to provide a great deal of interest in a very small space.*

Arched gateways tend to be rather suburban but that most useful variety of ivy, 'Goldheart', has been trained to cover the fence and archway, blending the whole structure into the adjoining border. Another attractive idea that would work well here would be to extend overhead beams out from the house. These would form a series of archways which could support climbers.

2   *Brash flower colour can often be the antithesis of good planting design. It would be difficult to fault this group of plants in any situation and it works particularly well against the clean lines of the adjoining house. Euphorbias are essentially 'architectural' plants, with their flower-like bracts. They associate well with a vast range of species, certainly adding emphasis to this particular composition of unusual plants.*

3 *This is essentially a plantsman's garden, with heavy emphasis on foliage rather than flower. Hostas again make their mark, while rodgersia, ferns, mahonia and rheum add breadth to the picture. Most of the plants shown are herbaceous perennials or deciduous shrubs, so in this particular garden the planting would provide little interest during winter. Fortunately, such species are fast growing and recover quickly each spring. They are invaluable in a young garden for adding instant maturity during the summer months. The yellow lilies are another herbaceous plant which provide spectacular summertime colour.*

Many broad-leaved plants look their best close to water, and in fact a high proportion of them enjoy moisture at their roots. Rheum and its giant cousin gunnera set up dramatic reflections. This too is the place for weeping willows – not in small front gardens where they quickly dominate everything. The timber deck forms an attractive path, but should preferably be constructed from a timber which is naturally resistant to damp conditions, or one which has been specially treated to resist dampness. It follows a gentle curve and the boards have been shaped accordingly. The gravel path provides simple access for maintenance.

1 *In this unquestionably Mediterranean garden, a high, walled courtyard is smothered in climbing plants. In this warm climate, pelargoniums are permanently planted outdoors where they can grow very large. How much better than having to bring them indoors each winter.*

The distribution of colour not only affects the way in which we look at a garden, but also tells us a good deal about personality. Hot colours – reds, oranges and vivid pinks – are dominant and produce spectacular restless compositions, so use them carefully and in tonal ranges. Bright light does much to temper a hot colour scheme, which is why municipal bedding displays look out of place when they use masses of tropical or sub-tropical plants in a temperate climate.

Bright annuals are often used to provide 'instant' colour. Try to plant them in drifts rather than in rigid ranks. If necessary, scatter seeds straight from the packet on to a prepared bed and thin out the plants as they come through.

Remember, too, that any garden can have a succession of year-round colour, from the earliest spring bulbs through to late-flowering Japanese anemones and asters. Colour schemes can therefore be planned in sequence, but do not forget to have a stable background of foliage.

1

2 *This garden uses a more limited range of colour, with two shades of pink in contrast to pure white. Astilbe, which forms the middle planting, is indispensable in any collection, its foliage being almost more attractive than its plumes of flower. It enjoys a cool root run and looks particularly good close to water.*

3 *Lavender* (Lavandula angustifolia) *and pale pink roses make up this typically English planting. Apart from the colour, this plant group will also be fragrant, adding another dimension to the garden designer's palette. Most fragrant plants are attractive to bees and butterflies as well. In this age of agricultural chemicals, many gardens provide a haven for insect life. The old yew hedge and brick steps are traditional features and the latter have been carefully built in a curving pattern. The shape is pleasing, but slightly impractical, as it is difficult to sweep.*

4 *Although it makes sense to work in either a hot or a cool colour range, the odd highlight can always prove attractive. The delicacy of this border is enhanced and highlighted by the splash of red roses. One of the jobs that can extend flowering times considerably is the removal of spent blooms, known as 'dead-heading'.*

1 *Monotone gardens with plants of one colour can either be bland or stunning. More often than not it is the former. There are, of course, exceptions. The famous White Garden at Sissinghurst in Kent is a superb case in point, where the monotone planting theme is one of several in a large garden whose success depends in part on the transition between one area and the next.*
Far more successful in a domestic situation is the provision of a corner or area which can be given over to planting along a single colour theme. This is precisely what has been done here and there is no doubt that white can be extraordinarily restful and elegant. Philadelphus acts as the background, its long arching branches laden with fragrant blossom. There are single and double forms of flower available; both are deliciously fragrant. White delphiniums can be more striking than the usual blue and here they lead the eye down to the old terracotta urn and simple paving of rectangular York stone. White-flowered Hosta elegans *spreads its broad leaves in the middle of the group, in direct contrast to the sword-like leaves of the yucca, another plant with white flowers.*
Although this example relies on flowers to carry the monotone theme, it is possible to work coloured foliage in as well.

1

2 *By using plants that grow close to the ground it is possible to reduce maintenance, especially weeding, to a minimal level. Such treatment over large areas is usually called 'ground cover' and can prove very effective. When choosing a species for ground cover, check its rate of growth. This planting is a combination of cotton lavender, stonecrop and violet.*

3 *Steps, raised beds and most hard landscaping benefit from the softening influence of plants. In fact, the one is not really complete without the other. Potentilla is a valuable species and most varieties grow in a carpeting pattern. One of the best known is Potentilla fruticosa 'Tangerine', shown here in full flower.*

4 *Ground cover need not necessarily take the form of shrubs or hardy perennials. Annuals can smother the ground very quickly. Here, white Marguerite daisies are teamed with pretty yellow African marigolds.*

5 *This soft and loose composition uses a wealth of different species to make up the overall concept. The density of the planting, rather than any one carpeting species, provides ground cover.*

1   *Trees are the biggest living things in the world and, apart from houses, they are usually the most dominant element in a garden. They take many years to develop and should be carefully chosen if they are not to grow out of proportion. This Robinia pseudoacacia 'Frisia', the golden-leaved robinia, is an ideal tree for the smaller garden with its stunning foliage. It does need shelter from high wind, as the branches are a little brittle.*

2   *Rhus typhina 'Laciniata', the stag's-horn sumach, is really a large shrub, but is big enough to act as a tree in many gardens. It has architectural line and the branches take on a sculptural air in winter. Its rich autumn colour is glorious, but this sumach does have an annoying tendency to send suckers to adjoining lawns.*

3   *This grouping of shade-tolerant plants is appropriate for its location on a wall that only catches very little sun in the late afternoon. The variegated philadelphus in the centre is plenty large enough in most borders, reaching 4.5m (15ft) in quick time.*

4   *This interesting combination of purple-leaved berberis (Berberis thunbergii 'Atropurpurea') and conifers is unusual but most effective, with minimal maintenance once established.*

PLANTING A TREE

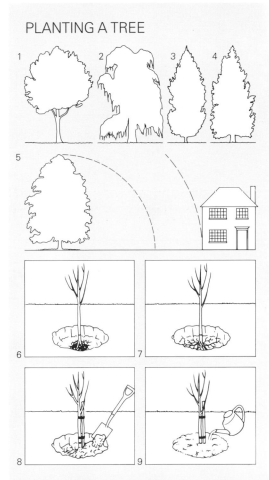

Trees have different growing habits, both in terms of shape and height. You can choose between trees of four types: **1** spreading, **2** weeping, **3** fastigiate and **4** conical. **5** In addition to selecting a tree which will not become too large, plant elm, oak, willow, poplar and cypress no closer to the house than one and a half times their mature height. **6** Dig a hole deep enough to plant the tree to the depth of the nursery mark on the stem and large enough to take the roots without cramping. Add leaf mould and peat before planting. **7** Trim off any damaged roots and spread the roots out. **8** Knock in a support, then fill in soil between the roots, firming as you go, up to the nursery mark on the stem. **9** After planting, water it well to settle the soil around the roots and speed growth.

5 *This attractive form of the common sycamore (Acer pseudoplatanus 'Brilliantissimum') has fine spring foliage, and this photograph shows it at its best, in May. Like most broad-leaved trees, it does cast heavy shade and this is always a point to be borne in mind when making a selection.*
Another consideration, if choosing a deciduous tree, is leaf fall, which in a well-treed garden can generate a great deal of work each autumn.

6 *This spring photograph shows the weeping whitebeam (Sorbus aria 'Pendula'), a tree tolerant of pollution and winds. Weeping trees are generally difficult to site in a garden as they are very obvious focal points. Most are too large for the small garden, but there are some good small-scale weeping trees available, including the willow-leaf pear, Pyrus salicifolia 'Pendula', and the weeping pussy willow, Salix caprea 'Kilmarnock'.*
The care of trees is no less important than the care of any other plant. The problem is that most people tend to forget about them. Regular feeding can certainly be beneficial, while the removal of dead or diseased timber is necessary to prevent the ingress of disease. The removal of a large tree is a job best left to expert professionals.

1 *Climbing plants are essential in any garden or backyard for a number of reasons. Perhaps most importantly, they can soften the line of overpowering boundaries. The smaller the garden, the more important this is. Plants may be grown against walls in small gardens where there is lack of space on the ground; they may enhance a building in some way. Climbing plants are also used to cover unsightly features. Climbing plants fall into two categories, those that cling to a wall (known as self-clingers) and those that need support. There is a third type that needs a wall to lean against, such as pyracantha or ceanothus, but these are really shrubs, not true climbing plants.*
There is a myth put about, largely by architects and engineers, that climbing plants harm a building. Generally this is not the case at all, but a thick mass of foliage could just hold a degree of moisture and cause dampness on a wall. Most climbers should never be allowed to form such dense growth and they usually benefit from selective thinning. They should also be kept clear from eaves and gutters, which can quickly become clogged with leaves. Hops, generally grown on a commercial basis for beer-making, are attractive as a garden twiner. Here, the golden form (Humulus lupulus 'Aureus') makes an attractive foil to brickwork.

1

2 *Ivies are self-clingers and one of the few climbing plants to thrive in really shady conditions. There are many types, from the broad-leaved* Hedera colchica *down to the smaller* Hedera helix *varieties. Here* Hedera helix *'Goldheart', whose variegated ever-gold foliage cheers up the coldest winter's day, has been trained to frame windows.*

3 Clematis montana *is one of the most valuable of the spring-flowering climbing plants. It is both vigorous and pretty, covering a wall or scrambling through a tree within two or three years after planting. The variety shown here is* Clematis montana *'Rubens', but there is a white-flowering form, 'Alba', which is equally attractive.*

4 *Virginia creeper* (Parthenocissus quinquefolia), *best known for its brilliant autumn foliage, is a self-clinging plant and one that can be grown in full shade. Chinese Virginia creeper (*Parthenocissus henryana) *has rich dark velvety-green or bronze leaves with veins picked out in pink and purple.*

5 *Honeysuckle (*Lonicera) *is the traditional sweet-smelling climber of country gardens. It flowers from June onwards and has a vigorous twining growth that is ideal for the face of a building or a pergola.*

1 *Vegetable gardening is above all a practical activity, but this is not to say that vegetable plants cannot contribute as much to a garden as strictly ornamental plants. On the Continent you can find them mixed up in the borders, contributing with their handsome foliage and often splendid flowers to the overall charisma of a garden. What could be more spectacular than a globe artichoke or a row of brilliant runner beans at the height of their flowering display? Even cabbages and in particular rhubarb can be interesting.*
All too often we relegate vegetables to a miserable patch tucked away in an obscure and out-of-the-way corner. Not only do we miss the joy of seeing them, but it is highly impractical to have to tramp long distances in the pouring rain to pull carrots. If vegetables are grown together in their own patch then access for maintenance is important, although stepping stones can be a nuisance. Far better to use paths, as shown here, and if these can be made attractive at the same time with a pattern of bricks or slabs, so much the better. Such paths can also form useful divisions for crop rotation or fruit.
The latter is another essential ingredient and in a small garden fruit trees or shrubs can often be grown on wires or against a wall to save space.

1

2   *This close-up view of the garden shown on the opposite page illustrates just how decorative vegetables can be. Runner beans and cabbages are at two ends of the vertical scale. There are a vast number of original ways to support beans, from fixing old bicycle wheels on to the top of poles to leaning old bedsteads together tent-fashion, and the results are superb.*

3   *This vegetable garden is of course pure pattern-making, and very successful it is too. In many ways it is reminiscent of a knot garden, but here the divisions are created with neat paths rather than hedges.*

4   *The old argument that herbs have no place in the vegetable garden is of little merit, especially when considering extremely small gardens with limited space. Herbs are certainly excellent in pots and a large strawberry pot, like the one shown here, is ideal. Tomatoes are another pot-loving plant. Indeed, it is quite feasible to grow most vegetables in containers.*

5   *In this very cosmopolitan garden, tomatoes, African marigolds and begonias all form a strictly regimented but colourful collection. This does in fact make excellent use of limited space and the wall could be neatly wired to support the tomatoes.*

1 *Whether grown in a patch dedicated to vegetables or nurtured in patio containers, food plants can be as decorative as strictly ornamental plants – an important consideration in a small garden. Look for varieties which will be as versatile as possible. For example, Swiss chard is immensely practical in a small garden. The wine-red leaves and crimson stem of rhubarb chard, the variety shown here, are decorative enough to feature in the border or a patio tub. New leaves, which taste like spinach, grow from the centre as the outer leaves are harvested for a good three months.*

2 *The ferny leaves of Florence fennel (also known as finocchio or anise) make an attractive backdrop to any planting – a double bonus for lovers of its faintly liquorice-flavoured bulb.*

3 *Fruit-bearing trees and vines, such as the handsome Chinese gooseberry (*Actinidia chinensis*) shown here, can be squeezed into a small garden by training them, like climbing plants, to cover a warm wall.*

4 *Globe artichokes, prized for the delicious 'heart' of their flower buds and for their superb silver-grey foliage, reward negligent gardeners with this spectacular thistle-like flower when they go to seed.*

5

6

7

5   There are many good reasons for growing food, even though fruits and vegetables are available year-round. Freshly picked fruits, herbs and vegetables are undoubtedly more flavourful, and there is a certain thrill to growing your own food, no matter how small the scale of production. Many cooks supplement store-bought produce by growing varieties which are not commercially cultivated. The long, thin Japanese aubergines shown here have thinner skins and milder, more delicate flavour than the globe-shaped ones.

6   For salad-lovers, cloches, like portable greenhouses, can extend the growing season, making it possible to pick a fresh salad throughout the winter. In a small garden, grow salad vegetables which are difficult to buy, such as the elegant Red Verona chicory (radicchio) shown here, corn salad (lamb's lettuce), endive and Chinese cabbages.

7   The custard marrows shown here (also called scallop or patty pan squashes) and golden courgettes, with their yellow flowers and fruit, look bold and gay. Both are delicious raw if harvested when extremely young, with the flowers still attached, although only more mature fruits are usually sold in stores.

1 *Herbs have played a vital role in both the development of gardens and man's social history. From the very earliest times the culinary and medicinal powers of herbs have been well known, and in Europe this knowledge has been systematically refined and developed for centuries, first in medieval monastic gardens and later in scientific 'physic gardens'. Many have healing powers that are still valued today. Although herbs are now mainly cultivated for cooking, they are also grown in contemporary gardens largely for their inherent beauty. They are on the whole a striking group of plants, often with superb foliage and an architectural line. The fact that they are also aromatic adds to their charm and it therefore makes sense to grow them close to a house where they can be enjoyed to the full and easily picked. Because many varieties are rampant, such as mint, it is sensible to grow these in pots where a vigorous root run can be held in check. Traditionally herbs have been grown in elaborate knot gardens, with individual species each allotted to a defined segment of the overall pattern. This delightful composition has been set out along similar lines in the shape of a wheel, the spokes of which separate the beds. Gravel paths provide access and a simple backdrop.*

2

3

4

2 *This type of pot is ideal for the less rampant varieties of herbs. Here a collection of basil, lemon balm, parsley and thyme is positioned close to a kitchen door for easy picking. The terracotta pot provides a cooler root run than plastic or metal. Regular watering is essential for any pot and particularly one that is set on a dry, hot, paved area. For this reason, large containers which retain more moisture are the best bet, particularly when you go away on holiday.*

3 *This pretty collection in a small domestic garden underlines the point that herbs can provide an enormous diversity of leaf and colour. Mint, marjoram, rosemary and parsley are all jumbled up together to give summer-long interest. This is the sort of collection where ruthless thinning is essential every couple of years.*

4 *Containers often start life as something else: this one was an old cattle manger. The fact that it is raised makes it easier to gather herbs and also gives a far better view from the adjoining windows. Old favourites and less common, though traditional, herbs are planted here, including sage, borage and thyme. All are handsome, and sage is particularly useful as it can have plain, variegated or multicoloured leaves.*

The naming and placing of plants within a garden is perhaps the most daunting task facing the amateur. Common plant names, although often easy to remember, are quite unreliable, and it is important to learn specialist nomenclature. The local name used for a plant in one part of the country could be totally different in another. It is important to know the whole name. *Viburnum davidii*, for example, is a ground-hugger, while *Viburnum rhytidophyllum* is a giant.

The guide to the top 100 plants for small gardens and backyards presented on the following pages can form the initial basis of a planting design. It lists a range of plants to provide an exciting and colourful array for all seasons, height ranges, formal and informal uses, floral effects, foliage effects and fragrance. Remember, though, that it is by no means comprehensive. One of the great joys of gardening is the discovery of new and unexpected delights that extend your knowledge of plants.

For ease of use, selected plants have been listed by type: trees; shrubs; perennials (long-lived plants which usually flower each year); annuals and biennials (plants which die or are discarded after flowering in their first or second year); and bulbs, corms and tubers. Some plants which are in fact perennial are often treated as annuals for practical purposes, and these have been listed along with the annuals and biennials. In addition, there are lists of perennial plants for water gardens and rock gardens. On page 71, there are index boxes to help you quickly find plants for any purpose.

The key features of each plant are described in abbreviated form: growing habit and type, size (height x spread, or height only), flowers and foliage, and a summary of growing requirements (hardiness and sun requirements). For trees and shrubs, the description will let you know whether the plant is deciduous (losing its leaves each winter) or evergreen.

KEY TO ABBREVIATIONS

ann.	annual	FR	fruits	S1	sun
bien.	biennial	LV	leaves	S2	sun/semi-shade
decid.	deciduous	per.	perennial	S3	semi-shade
evg.	evergreen	v.	very	S4	shade
FL	flowers	vars	varieties	S5	sun/shade

Hardiness (minimum temperatures)
H1   Extremely hardy −29°C (−20°F).
H2   Very hardy −18°C (0°F).
H3   Fairly hardy −6°C (21°F) to −15°C (5°F).
H4   Slightly hardy −6°C (21°F).
H5   Tender −1°C (30°F).

TREES

Acer pseudoplatanus 'Brilliantissimum' (sycamore var): slow-growing to 4.5×3.5m(15×12ft); LV decid., pinkish to yellow-green; H2; S1.

Betula pendula (silver birch): elegant and airy, to 9×4.5m(30×15ft); LV decid.; catkins, spring; white bark; H2; S1.

Crataegus monogyna 'Paul's Scarlet': to 6×6m(20×20ft); LV decid.; FL scarlet, late spring; FR red; H2; S1.

Chamaecyparis lawsoniana vars (Lawson's cypress): conifer, variable to 9m(30ft); LV evg., green, yellowish or grey/blue; H2; S1.

Eucalyptus gunnii (cider gum): to 15m(50ft) or more; LV grey, aromatic, whitish bark; FL cream, late spring; H2; S1.

Juniperus chinensis vars (Chinese junipers): to 4.5×1.2m(15×4ft); LV evg., greyish-green; H1; S1.

Laburnum × watereri 'Vossii' (golden rain tree): to 6×4.5m(20×15ft); LV decid.; FL yellow, spring; H2; S1.

Malus hybrids (crab apples): to 4.5-6×3-5.5m(15-20×10-18ft); LV decid., autumn colour; FL white/pink, spring; FR red/yellow; H2; S1.

Prunus hybrids (Japanese cherry): to 4.5×4.5m(15×15ft); LV decid., reddish when young, aut. colour; FL pink/white, spring; H2; S1.

Pyrus salicifolia 'Pendula' (willow-leaved pear): weeping, to 4.5×3.5m(15×12ft); LV decid., silver; FL cream, spring; H2; S1.

Robinia pseudacacia 'Frisia' (black locust var): to 12×6-9m(40×20-30ft); LV golden; dark bark; H1; S1.

Salix matsudana 'Tortuosa' (corkscrew willow): to 9×4.5m(30×15ft); LV decid.; catkins, spring; H2; S1.

Sorbus 'Joseph Rock': to 6×3.5m(20×12ft): LV decid., autumn colour; FL white, late spring; FR yellow; H2; S1.

Taxus baccata vars (yew): bushy, to 3.5×1.8m(12ft×6ft); LV, green/yellow; FR red/orange; H3; S5.

CLIMBING PLANTS

Chaenomeles × superba vars (flowering quince): 1.2×2.5m (4×8ft); LV decid.; FL red/pink/white, spring; FR yellow: H2; S1.

Clematis hybrids: 2.5-4.5m(8-15ft); LV decid.; FL large, purple/mauve/pink/white, spring/summer; H2; S5.

Hedera helix vars (ivy): to 9m(30ft); LV evg., green or cream/yellow; H2; S5.

Jasminum officinale (summer jasmine): to 9m(30ft); LV decid.; FL white, fragrant, summer; H3; S2.

Lonicera periclymenum (honeysuckle): to 6m(20ft); LV decid.; FL cream/purple, summer; FR red; H2; S3.

Pyracantha coccinea vars (firethorn): 2.5×2.5m(8×8ft); LV evg.; FL white, summer; FR orange/red; H2; S1.

Rosa hybrids (climbing rose): to 6m(20ft); LV decid.; FL red/pink/yellow/white, fragrant; H3; S1.

Vitis coignetiae (crimson glory vine): to 9m(30ft); LV decid., large, fine autumn colour; FR black; H2; S1.

SHRUBS

Aucuba japonica 'Variegata' (spotted laurel): to 3×3m(10×10ft); LV evg., yellow-spotted; FR red; H3; S4.

Berberis darwinii (barberry): to 3×3m(10×10ft); LV evg.; FL golden, spring; FR purple; H3; S3.

Berberis thunbergii vars: neat, 0.6-1.5×0.6-1.8m(2-5×2-6ft); LV decid., red-purple; FR red; H1; S1.

Buddleia davidii (butterfly bush): to 3×3m(7×7ft); LV decid.; FL lilac to purple, summer/autumn; H2; S7.

Camellia vars to 2×1.5m(7×5ft); LV glossy; FL large, pink/red/white, winter/spring; H3; S3; acid soil.

Choisya ternata (Mexican orange): 2×2m(7×7ft); LV glossy, evg; FL white, fragrant, spring; H3; S1.

Cotoneaster hybrids: to 1.8m(6ft); LV evg./decid.; FL cream, spring: FR red: H2/H3; S1.

Cytisus hybrids (broom): to 1.5×1.5m(5ft×5ft); LV decid.; FL cream/yellow/pink/red, spring/summer; H2; S1.

Euonymus fortunei vars: bushy/spreading, to 1×1.5m(3×5ft); LV evg.; often variegated; H2; S2.

Fatsia japonica (false castor-oil plant): bold, to 2×2m(7×7ft); LV evg., large; FL cream, autumn; H3; S3.

Fuchsia hybrids: bushy, to 1.2×1.2m(4×4ft); LV decid.; FL nodding bells, red/pink/purple, summer; H3; S1.

Hydrangea macrophylla: bushy, to 1.5×1.8m(5×6ft); LV decid.; FL pink/blue/white, summer; H2; S4.

Hypericum 'Hidcote' (St John's wort): bushy, to 1.5m×1.8m(5×6ft); LV decid.; FL golden, summer; H2; S1.

Lavandula spica (lavender): low/bushy, to 60cm(2ft), LV evg., grey; FL mauve/purple, summer; H2; S1.

Magnolia stellata (star magnolia): bushy, slow-growing to 2.5m(8ft); FL large, white, spring, H2; S1.

Mahonia japonica: upright, to 1.8×2.5m(6×8ft); LV evg.; FL yellow, fragrant, winter; FR bluish; H3; S4.

Philadelphus hybrids (mock orange): to 1.8m×1.8m(6×6ft); LV decid.; FL white, fragrant, summer; H2; S2.

Potentilla fruticosa hybrids: bushy, to 0.75-1.2×1-1.2m(2½-4×3-4ft); LV small, decid., greyish; FL cream/yellow/peach/red, summer/autumn; H1; S5.

Rhododendron hybrids (inc. Azaleas): size variable; LV evg./decid.; FL wide colour range, spring/summer; H1/H2/H3; S5; acid soil.

Rosa species & hybrids (rose): bushy, to 1.8×1.5m(6×5ft); LV decid.; FL red/pink/yellow/white, often fragrant, all summer; H2/H3; S1.

Skimmia japonica: bushy, to 1×1.5m(3×5ft); LV evg.; FL white, fragrant, spring; FR red, persistent; H3; S5; need cross-pollination.

Spiraea × bumalda 'Goldflame': to 60×90cm(2×3ft); LV decid., red to yellow; FL reddish, summer; H2; S1.

Syringa vulgaris (lilac): upright, to 3×2.5m(10×8ft); LV decid.; FL lilac/rosy-mauve/purple/white, fragrant, late spring; H1; S5.

Viburnum opulus (guelder rose): 2.5×1.8m(8×6ft); 'Compactum' dwarf; LV decid., autumn colour; FL white, spring; FR red/yellow; H1; S1.

PERENNIALS

Achillea 'Moonshine' (yarrow): to 60×45cm(2×1½ft); FL canary-yellow, early summer; H2; S1.

Anemone × hybrida vars (Japanese anemone): to 1-1.5×0.6m(3-5×2ft); FL pink/white, late summer to mid-autumn; H2; S1.

Aster novi-belgii vars (Michaelmas daisy): 0.3-1.2×0.3-0.45m(1-4×1-1½ft); mauve/purple/pink/red/white, autumn; H1; S1.

Astilbe × arendsii vars: 60-90×60cm(2-3×2ft); FL pink/red/white, summer; H2; S2; moist soil.

Bergenia hybrids: 30-45×30cm (1-1½×1ft); LV evg., winter colour; FL pink/white, spring; H1; S5; easy.

Chrysanthemum maximum (Shasta daisy): to 90×45cm(3×1½ft); FL showy, white, summer; H2; S1.

Cortaderia selloana 'Pumila' (dwarf pampas grass): 1.2m(4ft); FL cream, autumn; H3; sun.

Dryopteris filix-mas vars (male ferns): to 1.2×1m(4×3ft); H1; S5.

Epimedium pinnatum colchicum (bishop's hat): to 30×40cm(12×16in); FL, yellow; H2; S3; moist.

Eryngium × oliverianum (sea holly): to 1.5×0.6m(5×2ft); LV blue-green; FL mauve-blue, summer; H2; S1.

Euphorbia griffithii 'Fireglow' (spurge): to 75×60cm(2½×2ft); FL yellow/red bracts, spring/summer; H3; S1.

Geranium grandiflorum (cranesbill): to 30×60cm (1×2ft); LV autumn colour; FL mauve, summer; H2; S1.

Helleborus orientalis (Lenten rose): 45-60×45cm(1½-2×1½ft); LV evg.; FL cream to plum, winter; H1; S3.

Hosta hybrids (plantain lily): to 60-90×60cm(2-3×2ft); LV showy; FL white/violet, summer; H1; S5.

Lamium maculatum (spotted dead nettle): to 30×60cm(1×2ft); LV evg., marked silver; FL purplish, spring/summer; H1; S4.

Sedum spectabile (ice plant): to 45×45cm(1½×1½ft); LV grey-green; FL pink, autumn; H1; S1.

WATER PLANTS

Acorus calamus (sweet flag): 60-90cm (2-3ft); LV iris-like; H1.

Aponogeton distachyus (water hawthorn): 45cm(1½ft); LV green; FL white, spring-autumn; H4.

Caltha palustris (kingcup): to 30-40cm (12-16in); FL golden, spring; H1.

Eichhornia crassipes (water hyacinth): FL lavender-blue, summer; H5.

Iris laevigata (water iris): 45-75cm(1½-2½ft); FL blue-purple, summer; H2.

Nymphaea hybrids (water lily): spread to 1-1.5m(3-5ft); FL red/pink/yellow/white/, summer; H2.

Orontium aquaticum (golden club): to 45cm(1½ft), FL yellow; H2.

Pontederia cordata (pickerel weed): 60-90cm(2-3ft); FL blue; summer; H1.

Sagittaria sagittifolia (arrowhead): to 60cm(2ft), FL white, summer; H2.

Scirpus tabernaemontani 'Zebrinus': to 1m(3ft); LV banded white; H3.

BULBS, CORMS AND TUBERS

Agapanthus orientalis: to 1.2×0.6m(4×2ft); LV evg.; FL blue/white, summer; H4; S1.

Allium giganteum (giant onion): 1-1.5×0.3m(3-5×1ft); FL pink, summer; H2; S1.

Begonia x tuberhybrida: to 30×40cm(12×16in); FL vivid, summer; H5; S1.

Crocosmia × crocosmiiflora (mont-bretia): to 75×25cm (30×10in); LV semi-evg.; FL orange/red/yellow, summer; H3; S1.

Crocus vernus vars (Dutch crocuses): to 12cm(5in); FL purple/lilac/yellow/white, spring; H2; S1; easy.

Endymion hispanicus (Spanish bluebell): 30-45cm(1-1½ft); FL violet-blue, spring; H2; S5.

Galanthus nivalis (snowdrop): to 20cm (8in); FL white, winter; H1; S3.

Gladiolus × hortulanus: 1-1.2m(3-4ft); FL wide range, summer; H4/5; S1.

Hyacinthus orientalis (hyacinth): to 25-30cm(10-12in); LV strap-shaped; FL pink/blue/white/yellow, v. fragrant, spring; H2; S1.

Iris bearded hybrids: 40-120cm(16-48in); LV greyish, semi-evg.; FL wide range, summer; H2; S1.

Lilium regale (regal/royal lily): 1.2-1.8m(4-6ft); FL white, v. fragrant, summer; H1; S1.

Narcissus hybrids (daffodil): 35-45cm (14-18in); FL yellow, spring; H1; S5.

Tulipa hybrids (tulip): 25-60cm(10-24in); LV often greyish; FL vivid colour range, spring; H2; S1; easy.

ALPINE (ROCK GARDEN) PLANTS

Ajuga reptans (bugle): 10-30×45cm (4-12×18in); FL blue, summer; H1; S3.

Alyssum saxatile (gold dust): to 30×45cm(1×1½ft); FL golden, spring; H1; S1.

Aubrieta deltoides: to 15×60cm(6×24in); FL purple, spring; H2; S1.

Calluna vulgaris (heather): to 10-60×10-75cm(4-24×4-30in); LV coloured; FL pink/mauve/white, summer/autumn; H2; S1.

Campanula portenschlagiana (bellflower): to 15×60cm(6×24in); FL mauve-blue, summer; H2; S5.

Dianthus deltoides (pinks): 15-25×40cm(6-10×16in); LV evg.; FL red/pink/white, summer; H1; S1.

Gaultheria procumbens (creeping wintergreen): to 15×60cm(6×24in); LV evg.; FL white, summer; FR red; H1; S4.

Helianthemum nummularium vars (sun/rock rose): 15-30×60-90cm (6-12×24-36in); FL golden/pink/white, summer; H2; S1.

Phlox subulata (moss phlox): 10-15×45 cm(4-6×18in); FL pink, spring; H1; S1.

Saxifraga, mossy: 8-15×30-45cm (3-6×12-18in); FL pink, spring; H2; S3.

Sedum acre (stonecrop): 5×25cm (2×10in); LV evg.; FL yellow, summer; H2; S1.

Thymus serpyllum (thyme): 8×60cm(3×24in); LV evg.; FL crimson, summer; H1; S1.

ANNUALS AND BIENNIALS

Ageratum houstonianum (floss flower): bushy ann., 10-45×15-30cm(4-18×6-12in); LV hairy; FL blue/pink/white trusses, summer; H4; S1.

Alyssum maritimum (sweet alyssum): compact, bushy ann., 8-15×20-30cm(3-6×8-12in); FL profuse, white/lilac/purple, fragrant, all summer; H3; S1.

Antirrhinum majus maximum vars (snapdragon): shrubby per., grown as ann., to 75×45cm(2½×1½ft); FL in colours, summer; H4;S1.

Bellis perennis (English daisy): rosette per., grown as bien., to 10-15×15cm(4-6×6in); FL white/pink, mainly semi-double, spring/summer; H2; S1; easy.

Callistephus chinensis (China aster): bushy ann., to 20-75×30-60cm (8-30×12-24in); FL in wide colour range, summer; H3/H4; S1.

Dianthus barbatus (sweet William): upright bien., 15-60×15-25cm (6-24×6-10in); FL red/pink/white, often bicolours, summer; H2; S1.

Eschscholzia californica (California poppy): ann., 30-40×15cm(12-16×6in); LV greyish; FL orange/yellow/pink/red/white, summer; H2; S1.

Felicia bergerana (kingfisher daisy): mat-forming ann., to 20×15cm(8×6in); LV grey; FL steely-blue, yellow eye, summer; H4; S1.

Impatiens wallerana (busy Lizzie, patient Lucy): per., grown as ann., 15-60×25-45cm(6-24×10-18in); LV pale green/bronzed; FL white/pink/red/orange, summer; H4; S1.

Lavatera trimestris (annual mallow): bushy ann., to 1.2×0.45m(4×1½ft); FL pink/white, summer; H3/H4; S1.

Lobelia erinus vars (trailing lobelia): cascading ann., to 60cm(2ft); FL tiny, profuse, blue/purple/carmine/white, summer; H4; S1.

Lunaria annua (honesty): upright bien., to 75×30cm(2½×1ft); FL purplish, late spring; seed pods flat, silvery discs; H3; S1.

Myosotis sylvatica (forget-me-not): clump-forming bien., 15-40×15cm (6-16×6in); FL sky-blue/pink, spring; H3; S3.

Nemesia strumosa: ann., 20-30×15cm(8-12×6in); FL wide colour range, summer; H4; S1.

Pelargonium vars (regal, ivy & zonal geraniums): bed. per., to 45×40cm(18×16in); FL mauve/pink/white/red/orange, summer; H5; S1.

Petunia × hybrida: bushy ann., to 20-40×25cm(8-16×10in); FL in wide colour range, summer; H4; S1.

Tagetes patula (French marigold): bushy ann., to 20-30×30cm(8-12×12in); FL orange/bronze/yellow, summer; H4; S1; easy.

Verbena × hybrida (vervain): lax per., grown as ann., to 15-45×30cm (6-18×12in); FL vivid purple/red/pink, summer; H4; S1.

Viola × wittrockiana vars (pansies): compact ann./bien., 15-25×20-30cm(6-10×8-12in); FL flat, showy, wide colour range, often with 'faces', late spring/summer/winter; H3/H4; S3.

PLANTS WITH OUTSTANDING FOLIAGE

Acer tree	*Calluna* alpine	*Hedera* climber	*Robinia* tree
Ajuga alpine	*Chamaecyparis* tree	*Hosta* per.	*Spiraea* shrub
Aucuba shrub	*Epimedium* per.	*Juniperus* tree	*Taxus* tree
Berberis th. shrub	*Eucalyptus* tree	*Lamium* per.	*Viburnum* shrub
Bergenia per.	*Euonymus* shrub	*Pyrus* tree	*Vitis* climber

PLANTS FOR WINTER COLOUR

Aucuba shrub	*Euonymus* shrub	*Helleborus* per.	*Skimmia* shrub
Bergenia per.	*Galanthus* bulbs	*Juniperus* tree	*Taxus* tree
Chamaecyparis tree	*Gaultheria* alpine	*Mahonia* shrub	*Viola* ann./bien.

PLANTS FOR SPRING COLOUR

Acer tree	*Camellia* shrub	*Galanthus* bulbs	*Narcissus* bulbs
Alyssum sax. alp.	*Chaenomeles* climb.	*Hyacinthus* bulbs	*Phlox sub.* alp.
Aubrieta alpine	*Choisya* shrub	*Laburnum* tree	*Prunus* tree
Bellis ann./bien.	*Crataegus* tree	*Lunaria* bien.	*Rhododendron*
Berberis dar. shrub	*Crocus* bulbs	*Magnolia* shrub	*Syringa* shrub
Bergenia per.	*Endymion* bulbs	*Myosotis* bien.	*Tulipa* shrub

PLANTS FOR SUMMER COLOUR

Agapanthus bulbs	*Dianthus* alpine	*Jasminum* climb.	*Spiraea* shrub
Allium bulbs	*Fuchsia* shrub	*Lavandula* shrub	*Thymus* alpine
Begonia bulbs	*Gladiolus* bulbs	*Lilium* bulbs	See also:
Buddleia shrub	*Helianthemum* alp.	*Lonicera* climber	Annuals/bien.
Campanula alp.	*Hydrangea* shrub	*Philadelphus* shrub	Perennials
Clematis climber	*Hypericum* shrub	*Potentilla* shrub	Water plants
Crocosmia bulbs	*Iris* bulbs	*Rosa* shrub/climb.	

PLANTS FOR AUTUMN COLOUR

Acer tree	*Chaenomeles* climb.	*Epimedium* per.	*Sedum spect.* per.
Anemone per.	*Cortaderia* per.	*Malus* tree	*Sorbus* tree
Aster per.	*Cotoneaster* shrub	*Prunus* tree	*Viburnum* shrub
Berberis shrub	*Crataegus* tree	*Pyracantha* climb.	*Vitis* climber

PLANTS FOR CONTAINERS

Agapanthus bulbs	*Felicia* ann./bien.	*Lobelia* ann./bien.	*Tulipa* bulbs
Aucuba shrub	*Fuchsia* shrub	*Narcissus* bulbs	*Verbena* ann./
Begonia bulbs	*Hedera* climber	*Nemesia* ann./bien.	bien.
Camellia shrub	*Hyacinthus* bulbs	*Pelargonium* annual	*Viola* ann./bien.
Crocus bulbs	*Hydrangea* shrub	*Petunia* annual	
Euonymus shrub	*Impatiens* annual	*Rhododendron*	
Fatsia shrub	*Lilium* bulbs	shrub	

PLANTS FOR HANGING BASKETS

Begonia bulbs	*Hedera* climber	*Nemesia* annual	*Petunia* annual
Fuchsia shrub	*Lobelia* annual	*Pelargonium* ann.	*Verbena* annual

PLANTS FOR GROUND COVER

Ajuga alpine	*Epimedium* per.	*Hedera* climber	*Potentilla* shrub
Aubrieta alpine	*Euonymus* shrub	*Hosta* per.	*Saxifraga* alpine
Bergenia per.	*Gaultheria* alpine	*Lamium* per.	*Sedum acre* alp.
Campanula alp.	*Geranium* per.	*Phlox* alpine	*Thymus* alpine

SHADE-TOLERANT PLANTS

Ajuga alpine	*Endymion* bulbs	*Hydrangea* shrub	*Rhododendron*
Aucuba shrub	*Epimedium* per.	*Impatiens* annual	shrub
Bergenia per.	*Euonymus* shrub	*Lamium* per.	*Skimmia* shrub
Campanula alpine	*Fatsia* shrub	*Lunaria* ann./	*Taxus* tree
Clematis climber	*Gaultheria* alpine	bien.	
Dryopteris per.	*Hosta* per.	*Mahonia* shrub	

SCREENING & HEDGING PLANTS

Aucuba shrub	*Chamaecyparis* tree	*Crataegus* tree	*Rosa* shrub,
Berberis dar. shrub	*Cotoneaster* shrub	*Mahonia* shrub	climber
			Taxus tree

PRACTICALITIES

It is fair to say that any garden, however well designed, will need a degree of on-going maintenance. Wear and tear is bound to be a factor in hard landscape areas, while plants will need encouragement and pruning from time to time.

Tools and equipment are increasingly easy to care for, but always ensure that power equipment is regularly serviced, particularly electrical appliances. Hand tools work much more efficiently if kept sharp and lightly oiled, while timber fences and buildings need treating with non-toxic preservative every two years.

Good-quality, well-laid paving needs little attention, apart from sweeping down and keeping free from slime in pedestrian areas. For this, use a proprietary pool additive that discourages algae, watered down and swept over with a stiff broom. Occasionally, paving slabs get broken or bricks deteriorate owing to frost damage. They can be carefully chopped out using a hammer and bolster, then replacements laid in mortar to match the surrounding levels.

Walls, too, can show the effect of age, particularly in mature town gardens. Renovation will involve raking out the old joints, sweeping down and repointing. Provided it is otherwise sound, this will extend the life of a wall almost indefinitely.

Climbing plants, contrary to common belief, do little harm to a wall in good condition, but they may damage roofs and eaves. It is best to support climbers by horizontal wires spaced up the wall at 61cm (2ft) intervals. A trellis can often destroy the visual unity of a building and usually needs far more maintenance.

Pruning seems confusing to many people, but the rules are on the whole very straightforward.

Trees need thinning if they get too dense and any damaged or diseased branches should be carefully removed. Shrubs which flower in spring and early summer can be pruned after flowering, which means removing dead or weak growths and clipping over the more 'leggy' species. Later-flowering shrubs such as buddleia and hydrangea should be cut back in the spring so that young flowering stems can develop. Species such as the dogwoods (*Cornus*), which are planted for the winter interest of their stems, depend on new growth, and can be cut back hard in early spring during March.

HAND TOOLS CHECKLIST

- Spade(s) – choose between full-size digging spade and border spade. Stainless steel blades are more expensive than carbon steel.
- Fork(s) – choose between digging fork and border fork.
- Rake(s) – a lightweight head with about a dozen teeth will do for most soils. Fan-shaped rakes are good for lawn care.
- Hoe(s) – choose between long-handled Dutch-type hoe with a flat blade and draw hoe intended to be pulled backwards rather than pushed.
- Trowel – essential for planting.
- Shears – choose between long-handled edging and lawn shears and hedging shears.
- Secateurs – choose between curved- and straight-blade types.
- Hose.
- Hand sprayer.
- Watering can.
- Stiff broom.
- Wire and vine-eyes for supporting climbing plants.

This charming corner has it all: a barbecue area, log store and dining space set under the trees. This is simply good garden design: nothing contrived here, just sound common sense, which is precisely why it works so well.

Why should potting benches be both ugly and boring? This is a practical yet well-detailed corner which has been constructed from simple horizontal boards. It cleverly conceals an ugly concrete-block wall to the left while the roof is made of clear sheeting to admit maximum light.

Gardens have to contain the ugly as well as the beautiful and dustbins should always have a place to go. This store has been cleverly fitted into a bank and climbers soften its outline. It is close to the back door, so the timber has been stained to match that of the house.

Garden tools will give years of use, if you follow a few rules: never leave them outdoors when you have finished working; always clean and dry them after use; keep blades and fork tines lightly oiled; sharpen spades with an oil stone or a file occasionally and oil any wooden handles; always store in a dry place; only use tools on jobs for which they were intended.

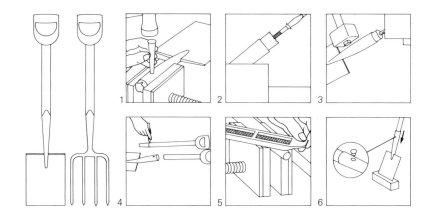

To replace a broken handle:
1 Punch out the rivet holding handle, working against the head. 2 Clamp spade in a vice, then drive a 152mm (6in) screw into broken end. 3 Holding the screw in a vice, tap the spade to release it. 4 Cut new handle to size. 5 Using a surform, taper the end to fit the spade socket. 6 Tap the handle home, then fit a screw to hold it in place.

Fence posts need to be really stable. To secure them you can set them into concrete 1, or you can add extra support with fence spikes 2 or concrete spurs 3 – both also excellent for repairing rotten or rickety posts. If you have many posts to sink, consider hiring or buying a post-hole borer 4 – but be warned, you need to be strong to use it!

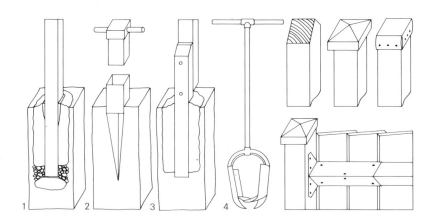

The tops of fence posts should be protected against rain penetration and eventual rotting. Do this by cutting the top with angled sides or by fitting special caps. The timber must have been treated against damp with a non-toxic preservative. To secure arris rails to fence posts, use angled arris rail brackets which have splayed ends for attaching to the post.

Make the most of walls in the garden by growing climbing plants over them, creating a living background for your garden. You will need to give the plants something to cling to, like a trellis, and most versatile is a trellis attached to a frame that is hinged at the base. This means you can swing it down to give access to the wall if you need to paint or repoint it at a later date.

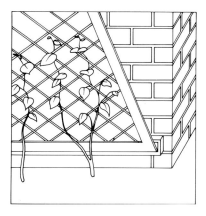

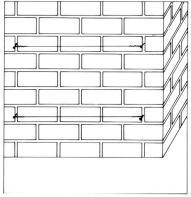

Another successful and less obtrusive way of growing climbers up a wall is to position horizontal wires at 305mm – 457mm (12in – 18 in) intervals for the plants to grow around. Wires should be about 76mm (3in) from the wall and attached by masonry nails or metal vine-eyes inserted into drilled and plugged holes to ensure that the full weight of the climber can be supported.

A glass or plastic tunnel cloche is ideal for protecting young plants against bad weather, helps speed growth and extends the growing season. Offering less protection but excellent for keeping off birds is a net cloche. Net can also be used with canes to form a 'tent' for sweet peas and runner beans to grow over, giving the plants maximum light and you easy access.

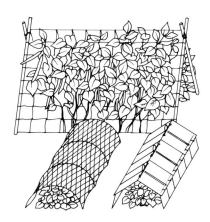

Perfect for patios, verandahs and greenhouses are grow-bags. Filled with a soil-less compost, these bags can support most flowers and vegetables, but are particularly good for tomatoes, beans and marrows. Always keep them well watered and fed though, as the compost can dry out very quickly in hot weather. Position them in a sunny place.

Supports come in all shapes and sizes, from crisp planed lengths of timber to the rustic poles shown here, and in all moods, from architectural to distinctly rural. The only problem with these poles is that they can rot quickly, particularly if the bark is left on.

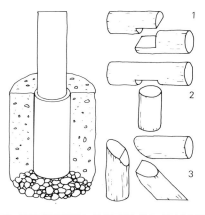

Construct an arbour using either squared timber or rustic larch poles. Secure in the ground by sinking in a section of plastic pipe positioned over hardcore, then embed in concrete. You can join lengths of larch pole with a halving joint 1; join verticals to horizontals by means of a notch in the cross beam 2; and use a birdsmouth notch 3 to fix a diagonal to a vertical post.

Using the right tools makes pruning easy. Long-handled pruners **1** give extra leverage for cutting through tough stems and are perfect for branches that are just out of arm's reach. For general work a pair of pruning shears or secateurs **2** are essential, but when you need greater control of the cut, use a pruning knife **3**. A selection of saws is necessary for trees.

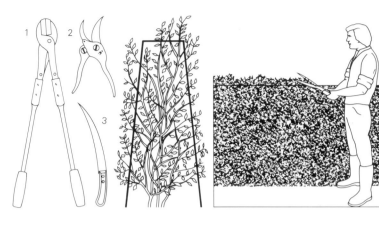

Clip hedges two or three times during the summer months using sharp, well-oiled shears. Shape so that the hedge is narrower at the top — this allows light to the base and helps to shed winter snow. To keep the top straight, stretch garden line between posts at the desired height, checking with a spirit level. Use this as a guide to work to but be careful not to cut through it.

Making a garden pool with a pond liner could be done in a weekend. **1** Mark out the required shape, including any marginal shelves, with a series of pegs and string. Dig out to this shape and firm down. **2** Use long battens and a spirit level to check the edges are level. Be sure to remove any sharp stones that could penetrate the liner, then cover the hollow with newspapers or

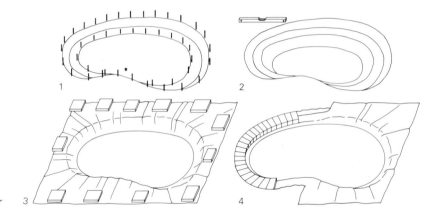

sand for extra protection. **3** Fit the liner into the hollow and secure at the perimeter with paving slabs or stones. Fill with water, the weight of which will fit the liner to the hollow. **4** Trim off any surplus liner, then bed decorative paving on to sand and cement to complete the pool edges. Plant out as desired, then leave the pool to settle and the water to clear, which may take a few weeks.

A permanent barbecue makes an interesting garden feature, plus it means the end of the storage problems caused by portables. If you're stuck for ideas, look out for DIY kits or copy this one with its variable grill heights, work space and storage area. Build against a wall, add a chimney and a small roof to protect against bad weather and you can use it throughout the year.

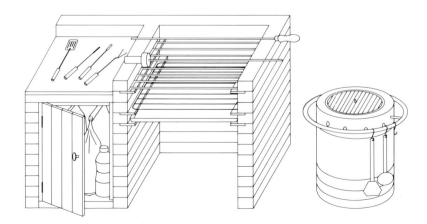

Oil drums have their uses and this has been made into a particularly sophisticated barbecue with vents and a circular hanging rail for utensils. Barrels and metal dustbins can likewise be converted into barbecues.

The lawnmower you opt for depends on the type and size of your lawn and the finished effect you want. For the classic striped effect a cylinder mower **1** is best – the more blades it has, the finer the cut, and this is important if you have a high-quality lawn. If you have an uneven lawn composed of rougher grass, a rotary mower **2** would be a better choice. If you have slopes to deal with a

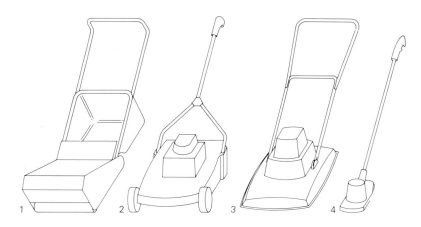

hover mower **3** is worth considering and these are ideal for those who lack the strength to deal with a heavier mower. A grass box can be an important addition if your lawn is large, as raking lawn clippings can take longer than mowing! Finally, for cutting edges and up to trees and fences there's a nylon thread trimmer **4** – easier and quicker than using edging shears.

Mow your lawn from March to October, judging frequency by growth. Never cut the grass too closely – to about 12mm (1/2in) minimum, but longer in dry spells to conserve moisture. Avoid mowing when the grass is wet – the end of the day is best – and don't leave cuttings on the lawn except in dry weather. Raking is necessary in spring and autumn to remove debris from the lawn.

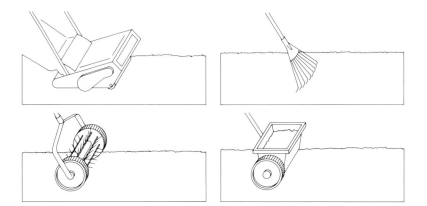

Aerating the lawn with a mechanical spiker or, on a smaller lawn, a fork, helps promote root growth and is essential for heavy or badly drained soils. Apply a light top dressing after aerating. For healthy lawn growth apply fertilizer in early April and later in the year, including an autumn feed, as necessary. A mechanical spreader distributes the fertilizer evenly.

Practicality is one of the keys to garden design and there is nothing more awkward or frustrating than having to mow close to a wall. By laying a course of bricks flat at the base of the wall you overcome this problem and create an attractive detail at the same time, as demonstrated by the graceful curved mowing strip illustrated here.

Removing a large bump or filling a hollow in a lawn is a relatively simple job but is best done between October and March. Using a knife, cut across the offending area, then gently ease back the turf. Remove excess or fill with top soil, then replace the turf and firm down. Fill in the cuts with sieved top soil. If the area is large, first cut turves from the centre, then fill or reduce as above.

INDEX

Page numbers in *italic* refer to illustrations and captions

ACKNOWLEDGEMENTS

The publisher thanks the following photographers and organizations for their kind permission to reproduce the photographs in this book:

Heather Angel **26** *1*, **27** *6*, **30-1**, **39** *2*, **50** *3*, **52** *2*, **52-3** *3*, **60** *1*: ARCAID (Richard Bryant) **26** *3*, **28** *2* (John Croce) **6-7** *3*; Michael Boys **8** *3*, **24** *2*, **44** *1*; Linda Burgess **25** *5*, **34** *2*, **46** *3*; Camera Press **9** *4*, **11** *2*, **27** *4*, **35** *10*; Inge Espen-Hansen **63** *4*, **67** *4*; Robert Estall **16-17** *1*; John Glover **27** *7*; Good Housekeeping (Jan Baldwin) **42-3** *1* (Hugh Palmer) **63** *3*; Derek Gould **67** *2*; Pamela Harper **27** *5*; Jerry Harpur **19** *2*, **25** *6*, **35** *9*, **45** *3*, **48-9**, **50** *2*, **57** *5*, **63** *5*, **66-7** *1*, **67** *3* (designer Mackenzie Bell) **4-5** (designers Hillier & Hilton – Helen and Desmond Preston's garden) **14** *1* (Don Drake) **15** *2* (Geoff Kaye, Clifton Nurseries) **25** *4*, **34** *4* (Hillier & Hilton) **34** *5* (Vic Shanley, Clifton Nurseries) **35** *7*, **39** *3* (John Brookes) **35** *12* (Alan Mason, Harewood) **55** *2* (Barnsley House, Cirencester) **62** *1*, **63** *2*; Marijke Heuff, Amsterdam **10** *1* (Yak Ritzen, Holland) **26** *2*, **34** *6* (Wim Lansonder, Holland) **38-9** *1* (Mr & Mrs van Bennekom-Scheffer, Holland – garden open to public 1st weekend in July) **40** *1* (Mien Ruys & Hans Veldhoen, Holland) **40** *2*, **50** *4* (André van Wassenhove, Belgium) **40-1** *3*; Neil Holmes **1**, **6** *1*, **19** *4*, **35** *8*, **55** *3*, **64** *1* and *2*; Pat Hunt **34** *3*; Jacqui Hurst **24** *1*; Impact Photos/Pamela Toler **47** *4*; Michelle Lamontagne **8** *2*, **17** *2* and *3*, **18** *1*, **33** *2*, **36** *1*, **37** *2*; George Lévêque **28** *1*, **29** *5*, **32** *1*, **33** *3*, **47** *6* (architect Michel Renévot) **32** *1*, La Maison de Marie Claire (Viane/Belmont) **24** *3*; Peter McHoy **28** *3*, **46** *1*, **47** *5*, **52** *1*; Tania Midgley **35** *11*, **56-7** *1*; Mon Jardin et Ma Maison/Kolko **72-3** *1*; Octopus (Michael Boys) **58** *2*, **61** *3*, **64** *4* (Jerry Harpur) **55** *4*, **58** *1*, **58** *4*, **59** *5* and *6*, **61** *2*, *4* and *5* (George Wright) **51** *5*, **57** *2* and *3*; Philippe Perdereau **19** *5*, **28** *4*, **50** *1*, **54** *1*, **75**; Photos Horticultural **12-13** *1*, **65** *5*, *6* and *7*; Harry Smith Horticultural Collection **64** *3*; David Stevens **45** *2* and *4*, **46** *2*, **57** *4*, **58** *3*, **74** *1* and *2*, **77**; Elizabeth Whiting & Associates **34** *1* (Michael Dunne) **8** *1* (Michael Nicholson) **6** *2* (Jerry Tubby) **19** *3*.

Source material for the following illustrations was supplied by Homebase:
33, **59**, **74** above, **75** above and centre, **76** above, **77**.